The Word Of God Library™

God's Prophetic Word Through Amos

Roger Henri Trepanier

This book, and all the author's books, are available for purchase in print format or as an e-Book on all major distribution channels. Since the author's two websites are no longer active, one may access the books, and places to purchase, by typing "Roger Henri Trepanier, books" in any search engine.

This book is dedicated to Meno Kalisher, senior minister of the Jerusalem Assembly in Israel.

“shepherd the flock of God among you, exercising oversight not under compulsion, but voluntarily, according to the will of God; and not for sordid gain, but with eagerness; nor yet as lording it over those allotted to your charge, but proving to be examples to the flock. And when the Chief Shepherd appears, you will receive the unfading crown of glory.”

1 Peter 5:2-4

Titles available from Roger Henri Trepanier in The Truth Seeker's Library™ series:

God Did Not Create Human Beings To Die... But To Live On... Eternally!
Finding Comfort And Encouragement In The Promises Of God In The Last Days
How We Know For Sure That We Are Living In The Last Days!
Have You Ever Wondered What Happens After Death?
An Introduction To The New World That Is Coming On The Earth
Deeper Truths Of The Christian Life
Evangelism As God Intended
Keeping On Serving God In The Last Days
The Mysterious World Of Angels And Demons
No One Loves As He Loves!
Thanks Be To God For His Indescribable Gift!
The Church Is Very Much Alive, Well, And Growing!
Tracing The Steps Of The Son Of God From Eternity To Eternity!
War, And Going To War, Is Simply Not Of God!
God Never Meant Prayer To Be A Mystery!
Health Is One Of God's Great Blessings!
Removing The Mystery Surrounding Baptism!
This World's Return To Paganism Is Almost Complete!
Removing The Mystery Surrounding Heaven!
God's Covenants Were Meant For Mankind's Blessing!
The Four Ages Of Time
The Awesomeness Of God!
A Call To A Biblical Christianity!
Believers! Look Up! Our Homegoing Is Any Day!
Why God Created The Male And The Female!
This Earth Was Never Meant To Be The Believer's Home!
It Is A Terrifying Thing To Fall Into The Hands Of The Living God!
The Rapture Of The Church Is God's Last End Time Event!
This Present Earth Will One Day Be Eternal Hell!
The Importance Of The Son, To God The Father And To All Believers!
Questions That God Wants Answers To!
The Danger Of Being A Christian In Name Only, Or Not At All!

Titles available from Roger Henri Trepanier in The Practical Helps Library™ series:

Learning to Overcome The Perplexities Of This Present Life
So, I Hear You Want To Work With Seniors?
I Will Not Have This Man To Rule Over Me!
Spiritual Truth To Warm The Heart!
Fasten Your Seatbelts: Turbulence Ahead!
Living A Normal Christian Life In An Increasingly Abnormal World!
If You Have Jesus; You Do Not Need Drugs!
To Do God's Will Is To Have A Foretaste Of Heaven!
This World Is Ready For The Rule Of The Antichrist!
President Trump And The Q Movement Versus Satan And The DEEP STATE
More Of God's Great Promises For Comfort And Encouragement!
Alert! The C-Virus Pandemic Was Satan's Practice Run For A New World Order
The Days Are Evil! The Time Is Short! Be Saved From This Perverse Generation!
Your Worldview Determines Your Wellbeing And Eternal Destiny!
What We Are Watching Is The Spirit Of The Antichrist At Work!
A Sure Cure For Loneliness!
Will God Allow President Trump To Regain The White House?
The Antichrist Arises Out Of Europe And Is About To Appear On The World Scene!
Helping Believers Live In A World With No Normal!
Sorry! America Will Never Be Great Again!

Titles available from Roger Henri Trepanier in The Christian Fiction Library™ series:

The Beginning Of A New Dawn
It Is Never Too Late For Love!
The True To Life Musings Of Fred And Ernie
Between A Rock And A Hard Place!
Love Knows No Boundaries!
A Woman Worth Pursuing!
Love Is More Than Just A Four Letter Word!
The Twists And Turns Of The Life Of Faith!
Even A Match Made In Heaven Must Be Outworked On Earth!

Titles available from Roger Henri Trepanier in The Word Of God Library™ series:

God's First Letter To The Thessalonians
God's Second Letter To The Thessalonians
God's Letter To Believers Through Jude
God's Three Short Letters To Believers Through John
God's Letter To Scattered Believers Through James
God's Letter To Titus
God's Prophetic Word To Mankind Through Daniel
God's Letter To Philemon And God's Letter To The Colossians
God's Consummation Of All In The Book Of Revelation
God's Letter To The Philippians
God's First Letter Through Peter
God's Second Letter Through Peter
Jonah, God's Reluctant Prophet!
God's Letter To The Galatians
God's Providence In The Book Of Esther
God's Love For Gentiles In The Book Of Ruth
God's Letter To The Ephesians
God's First Letter To Timothy
God's Second Letter To Timothy
Jesus' Sermon On The Mount: Matthews 5 to 7
Jesus" Parting Words Of Love To His Own: John 13 To 16
God's Letter To The Romans Through The Apostle Paul
God's Letter To The Hebrews
God's First Letter To The Corinthians
God's Second Letter To The Corinthians
God's Prophetic Word Through Malachi
God's Word Through Ezra
God's Word Through Nehemiah
God's Prophetic Word Through Haggai And Zechariah
God's Prophetic Word Through Micah

INTRODUCTION

God is allowing His servant to have a few commentaries published, which are the product of over forty-three years of study and experience. It is my hope that the present one, "God's Prophetic Word Through Amos" – which is expository in nature (that is, explained in detail) – will prove to be heartwarming and practical to help God's people live in a way that is a personal blessing and which brings glory to God in these last days of the present age!

There are three things that one should be aware of at the outset. The first is that the Bible text that God gave will be included as part of the text of this book, so that the reader will not have to turn to the Bible to read that text. It will appear in italics. Then secondly, each chapter has been broken into smaller sections, which will begin with an italicized brief explanation supplied as a help of what is covered in that section. And thirdly, at times comments are supplied by the author, which will be in brackets in the text of God's word, as an additional help to the reader.

It should be noted that there is an Addenda at the back of the book with five sections. In Addendum A, there is a brief outline of the four ages of time, for any reading the book who might not be familiar with this information. In Addendum B, there is a brief outline of the two comings from Heaven to earth in time of God's Son, The Lord Jesus Christ. In Addendum C, we have an exposition on how and for what purpose God raised up the nation of Israel in time. In Addendum D, we have an exposition on the nature of man and the consequence of sin, and then in Addendum E we have a presentation of the gospel, which is the good news that God has given in His word regarding His Son, The Lord Jesus Christ, for any reader who might not yet have this vital personal relationship with God, through faith in His Son.

What should also be mentioned before closing this Introduction, because we are all somewhat curious by nature, is that after completing 21 years of formal education and then spending almost 28 years working in Project Engineering and Management in the Corporate offices of two large utilities, God called His servant as a non-denominational evangelist in early 1999, and then sent him out over two thousand miles, away from family and friends, to the place of service God assigned, which is where His servant has been, and is still serving Him, as evangelist, author, and counselor. The author is a widower with three adopted children, all now married with a family of their own.

This book, and all the author's books, are available for purchase in print format or as an eBook on all major distribution channels. Since the author's two websites are no longer active, one may access the books, and places to purchase, by typing "Roger Henri Trepanier, books" in any search engine.

And now my prayer is that God will richly bless you as you read this book, and greatly minister to every need in your life, as only God can! To Him be all praise, honor, and glory, with thanksgiving, both now and forevermore! Amen.

CONTENTS

CHAPTER ONE

Amos 1:1-15

Verse 1:1, Introduction

As we begin, let us note what God tells us at Amos 1:1, which is God's introduction to His prophetic word through Amos, where we read, *"The words of Amos, who was among the sheepherders from Tekoa, which he envisioned in visions concerning Israel in the days of Uzziah king of Judah, and in the days of Jeroboam son of Joash, king of Israel, two years before the earthquake."*

There are a number of truths that God makes known in His introduction, as He begins His prophetic word through Amos. The first truth is that God tells us that He gave this word through Amos, even though at verse 1:1 we read, "The words of Amos." This simply meant that Amos was the one that God spoke through, and who then wrote this down for the benefit of all mankind.

Let us note some verses of God's word to help us here in this regard, the first being what we read at Acts 3:21, "whom heaven must receive until the period of restoration of all things about which GOD SPOKE BY THE MOUTH OF HIS HOLY PROPHETS from ancient time," then also at Hebrews 1:1, where we read, "GOD, AFTER HE SPOKE long ago to the fathers IN THE PROPHETS in many portions and in many ways...," and then at 1 Peter 1:20,21, "[20] But know this first of all, that no prophecy of Scripture is a matter of one's own interpretation, [21] for no prophecy was ever made by an act of human will, BUT MEN MOVED BY THE HOLY SPIRIT SPOKE FROM GOD."

A second truth God tells us is that Amos, "was among the sheepherders from Tekoa." In other words, when God first came to Amos to start speaking His word through Him, Amos was a shepherd of literal sheep. We later see at Amos 7:14 that Amos did not want to be regarded as a prophet, but was content to be seen as a herdsman and a grower of figs.

A third truth that God then tells us is that Amos was from Tekoa, which was a town in Judah, about six miles south of Bethlehem. Rehoboam, who became king over Judah after king Solomon's death, built fortified cities in Judah, with one of them being at Tekoa, noting 2 Chronicles 11:1-10.

A fourth truth God mentions from verse 1:1, and which also forms part of this introduction, is that Amos was given "visions." In other words, God's way of communicating His word to mankind through Amos was by means of visions. Let us note what God says at Numbers 12:6 in this regard, "Hear now My words: If there is a prophet among you, I, the Lord, shall make Myself known to him in a vision. I shall speak with him in a dream," and also at Hosea 12:10, "I have also spoken to the prophets, and I gave numerous visions, and through the prophets I gave parables."

Then a fifth truth that God gives here is that it was "concerning Israel," that God was now giving this prophetic word through Amos. What is important to grasp is that when God says, "Israel" here, He is speaking about the Northern kingdom part of the nation of Israel, although at times God does address the Southern kingdom of Judah also, and at other times the nation of Israel as a whole, meaning both the Southern kingdom of Judah and the Northern kingdom of Israel together.. What would be useful at this point is to provide a little background information for those readers who may not be too familiar with the history of the nation of Israel.

What is important to know and keep in mind here then is that from after the time of king Solomon, we have the nation of Israel being divided into two kingdoms, which will remain divided until after the second stage of the second coming of God's Son during the fourth age of time. Those two kingdoms that the nation of Israel was divided into was the Southern kingdom of Judah, consisting of the tribes of Judah and Benjamin, with its capital at Jerusalem, which was in Judah; while the other kingdom was the Northern kingdom of Israel, which consisted of the remaining ten tribes, with its capital being at Samaria, which was in Ephraim.

In 722 BC, the Northern kingdom of Israel was brought into captivity to Assyria and the territory of the ten tribes was then repopulated with foreign people, as we see from 2 Kings 17:6,24. And then in 586 BC, the Southern kingdom of Judah was brought into captivity to Babylon, under its first king, Nebuchadnezzar, with the city of Jerusalem, including God's temple there, being burned to the ground at that time. It is important to grasp that both the Northern Kingdom of Israel and the Southern Kingdom of Judah were exiled from the land of Israel by God due to their sin against God, as is clear from 2 Kings 17:7-23!

What should also be noted here is that in God's book of Daniel, He there prophesied four world-encompassing empires of men in unbelief in time, with the first world empire being that of Babylon, with its capital at the city of Babylon; the second being that of Persia and Media, with its capital at Susa; the third being that of Greece, with its capital at Athens; and then the fourth being the Roman empire, with its capital at the city of Rome.

And so, coming back to God's prophetic word through Amos, the sixth truth that God shares with us is that He led Amos to prophesy "in the days of Uzziah king of Judah, and in the days of Jeroboam son of Joash, king of Israel, two years before the earthquake." In other words, these were the kings who were ruling in Israel during the time that Amos was led of God to prophesy to the Northern kingdom of Israel. Amos himself, being from Tekoa, in Judah, went to the Northern kingdom of Israel to prophesy against it there, noting Amos 7:12,13.

Since we are specifically told that it was two years before the earthquake, which is also mentioned at Zechariah 14:5, then we know that Amos prophesied within a one year time frame, Biblical scholars believe this earthquake occurred in 760 BC, which therefore means that Amos would have prophesied in 762 BC. We need to remember that the years decline as we go forward to the time of the appearance of God's Son on earth. BC here means 'Before Christ.' This was about 40 years before the exile of the Northern kingdom of Israel to Assyria, which occurred in 722 BC.

Before leaving this introduction, we should speak briefly about king Uzziah of the Southern kingdom of Judah and king Jeroboam of the Northern kingdom of Israel. God gives us a good account of the reign of king Uzziah of Judah at 2 Chronicles 26:1-23. Briefly, we can say here that he came to power at 16 years of age, after succeeding his father Amaziah to the throne, and reigned for 52 years in Jerusalem. He was a believer, but later in life he became proud and incurred the judgment of God, who gave him leprosy, with which he died.

As to king Jeroboam of the Northern kingdom of Israel, we can briefly note what God says of him at 2 Kings 14:23,24, "[23] In the fifteenth year of Amaziah the son of Joash king of Judah, Jeroboam the son of Joash king of Israel became king in Samaria, and reigned forty-one years. [24] He did evil in the sight of the Lord; he did not depart from all the sins of Jeroboam the son of Nebat, which he made Israel sin."

What is important to keep in mind as we continue is that the Northern kingdom of Israel was in unbelief from the time that the nation of Israel was divided into two kingdoms after the time of king Solomon. God kept sending prophets to them to bring them to faith in Him, such as Amos, but it would be to no avail, as the Northern kingdom would remain in unbelief until its exile to Assyria in 722 BC.

Amos 1:2, a general statement of fact by God through Amos

We then note from Amos 1:2 that God leads Amos to give a general statement of fact, with the *"He said"* here being in reference to Amos, who was led of God to say, *"The Lord roars from Zion and from Jerusalem He utters His voice; and the shepherds' pasture grounds mourn, and the summit of Carmel dries up."*

We are to see that "Zion" here was a reference to the temple mount, where The Lord's temple stood that had been built through king Solomon, noting 1 Kings 6:1; Psalm 51:18,19; and Isaiah 12:6. This was where God's Presence was on earth, from the Holy of holies of that temple, as we further see from Leviticus 1:1; Exodus 25:22; and Numbers 7:89.

And when we read here that “the Lord roars,” this is to indicate that just as a lion roars before leaving the den to hunt, as a warning to all the prey in his surroundings, so too is God here pictured as about to bring His judgment on the Northern kingdom of Israel, noting Isaiah 31:4 and Hosea 11:10. And because this is so, then there are two things that are affected by this coming judgment, the one being that God’s judgment will result in the pasture ground of the shepherds mourning and also the high ground of Mount Carmel drying up, with both being in the territory of the Northern kingdom of Israel. The likely judgment in view here would be exile of the Northern kingdom to Assyria in 722 BC, which would then leave the pasture grounds without sheep to graze, and high ground of Mount Carmel dry due to lack of rain, which God knows would not be needed, due to the people having been exiled!

We should also state a truth which is important for us to remember here as we proceed in God’s prophetic word through Amos, which is for us to keep in mind that the nation of Israel during the second age of time was but a representative nation of all the nations on earth. What this means is that whatever God says about the nation of Israel in His word, would have been said also had any other nation been chosen by God instead as a representative nation!

What this further means is that when Israel is seen sinning against God and being rebellious, whether that be the Southern kingdom of Judah or the Northern kingdom of Israel, any other nation chosen instead of Israel would have done exactly the same sin in the same situations. And so, whatever judgment God pronounces against Israel in His word is deserved by ALL NATIONS ON EARTH, for as God says at Romans 3:23, “for all have sinned and fall short of the glory of God.”

Amos 1:3-5, God prophesies His coming judgment against Damascus

After speaking in veiled terms of judgment to come against the Northern kingdom of Israel at verse 1:2, God now turns His attention to a surrounding nation, namely Syria, with Damascus as its capital, and now pronounces judgments on it, as we now see from Amos 1:3-5, where we read, *“[3] Thus says the Lord, "For three transgressions of Damascus and for four I will not revoke its punishment, because they threshed Gilead with implements of sharp iron. [4] So I will send fire upon the house of Hazael and it will consume the citadels of Ben-hadad. [5] I will also break the gate bar of Damascus, and cut off the inhabitant from the valley of Aven, and him who holds the scepter, from Beth-eden; so the people of Aram will go exiled to Kir," says the Lord."*

We get a clear example here at verse 1:3, in the words, "Thus says the Lord," that Amos was simply called of God to be God's mouthpiece for Him to speak through and then to record for posterity what God said And so, we are to see all Scripture as being God's word, and not in any way that of any human being, noting for instance what we read at 2 Timothy 3:16, "All Scripture is inspired by God (God-breathed) and profitable for teaching, for reproof, for correction, for training in righteousness..."

Then we are to note that when God says at verse 2:3 here, and elsewhere in this prophetic word, "For three transgressions... and for four I will not revoke its punishment," God is simply using these terms in a manner of speaking, to point out that His judgment was coming on them and would not be revoked, due to there being multiple transgressions for which they were guilty before God! In other words, what Syria did to the nation of Israel is like the "unpardonable sin" that God's Son mentions at Matthew 12:31,32!

And one such sin that Syria committed, which God ascribes to Damascus, its capital and seat of power, is that "they threshed Gilead with implements of sharp iron." God is using terminology here that all those reading this at the time of Amos would have understood, for when grain was threshed to separate the grain from its husk, a heavy wooden sledge with iron teeth would be pulled over the grain. Now God uses this to illustrate what the Syria, as represented by Damascus, has done to the nation of Israel during its history so far.

God then mentions two individuals at verses 1:4 here, namely Hazael and Ben-hadad, who will suffer at God's Hand in the coming days. And what we are to note here is that Syria was here now being seen as being under the rule of Aram at this time, so that both Ben-hadad and Hazael, who were two kings of Aram, were stationed in Damascus when they did great damage to the nation of Israel.

We would benefit in noting the encounter of the prophet Elisha with both these men at 2 Kings 8:7-15, as background information here, "[7] Then Elisha came to Damascus. Now Ben-hadad king of Aram was sick, and it was told him, saying, "The man of God has come here." [8] The king said to Hazael, "Take a gift in your hand and go to meet the man of God, and inquire of the Lord by him, saying, 'Will I recover from this sickness?' " [9] So Hazael went to meet him and took a gift in his hand, even every kind of good thing of Damascus, forty camels' loads; and he came and stood before him and said, "Your son Ben-hadad king of Aram has sent me to you, saying, 'Will I recover from this sickness?' " [10] Then Elisha said to him, "Go, say to him, 'You will surely recover,' but the Lord has shown me that he will certainly die." [11] He fixed his gaze steadily on him until he was ashamed, and the man of God wept. [12] Hazael said, "Why does my lord weep?" Then he answered, "Because I know the evil that you will do to the sons of Israel: their strongholds you will set on fire, and their young men you will kill with the sword, and their little ones you will dash in pieces, and their women with child you will rip up." [13] Then Hazael said, "But what is your servant, who is but a dog, that he should do this great thing?" And Elisha answered, "The Lord has shown me that you will be king over Aram." [14] So he departed from Elisha and returned to his master, who said to him, "What did Elisha say to you?" And he answered, "He told me that you would surely recover." [15] On the following day, he took the cover and dipped it in water and spread it on his face, so that he died. And Hazael became king in his place."

Then when God says at verse 1:5 that He will "break the gate bar of Damascus," He is indicating that in His judgment to come, which will be at the hands of the Assyrians, Damascus, which was a fortified city with walls and gates, would be overthrown! We see that occurring in 732 BC, when Assyria came against Damascus, as we read at 2 Kings 16:7,9, "[7] So Ahaz sent messengers to Tiglath-pileser king of Assyria, saying, "I am your servant and your son; come up and deliver me from the hand of the king of Aram and from the hand of the king of Israel, who are rising up against me… [9] So the king of Assyria listened to him; and the king of Assyria went up against Damascus and captured it, and carried the people of it away into exile to Kir, and put Rezin to death." This was ten years before the exile to Assyria of the Northern kingdom of Israel, which took place in 722 BC.

The places we also see mentioned at verse 1:5, namely "the valley of Aven" and "Beth-eden" are not mentioned in the Bible and are most likely places in Aram, which would also experience God's judgment when Assyria comes as God's instrument of judgment. And when we read at verse 1:5 that "the people of Aram will go exiled to Kir," God is again indicating that this will occur at the hands of Assyria. We see from Amos 9:7 that Kir, which was in Assyria, was where the Arameans that were now in Syria had come from. And now God was having them go back there as part of His judgment!

Amos 1:6-8, God prophesies His coming judgment against Gaza

As we then see from Amos 1:6-8, God continues to prophesy through Amos His coming judgment against surrounding nations, this time focusing on Gaza, as we now see, *"[6] Thus says the Lord, "For three transgressions of Gaza and for four I will not revoke its punishment, because they deported an entire population to deliver it up to Edom. [7] So I will send fire upon the wall of Gaza and it will consume her citadels. [8] I will also cut off the inhabitant from Ashdod, and him who holds the scepter, from Ashkelon; I will even unleash My power upon Ekron, and the remnant of the Philistines will perish," says the Lord God."*

We are to see here that Gaza was the capital of the Philistine territory, with some of its cities being mentioned here, such as Ashdod, Ashkelon, and Ekron. And what God was especially angry at Gaza for is that it sat on major trade routes, with one passing through the territory of the Edomites, and so as the Philistines carried out raids into Israelite territory, they would take the people captive and sell them to the Edomites, who then sold them as slaves throughout the world.

God alludes to this at Joel 3:4-6, where we read, "[4] Moreover, what are you to Me, O Tyre, Sidon and ALL THE REGIONS OF PHILISTIA? Are you rendering Me a recompense? But if you do recompense Me, swiftly and speedily I will return your recompense on your head. [5] Since you have taken My silver and My gold, brought My precious treasures to your temples, [6] AND SOLD

THE SONS OF JUDAH AND JERUSALEM TO THE GREEKS IN ORDER TO REMOVE THEM FAR FROM THEIR TERRITORY..."

And as a result, God here prophesies through Amos that His judgment would fall on all the territory of the Philistines, which judgment God would again be bringing against them at the hands of the Assyrians. When God says at verse 1:8, "the remnant of the Philistines will perish," He is here indicating that He will one day totally wipe out the Philistines from the annals of history, in that there will not be any remnant of them left anywhere!

We further note that God has so far identified Himself as simply, "the Lord" (Yahveh), noting verses 1:2,3,5,6; but here at verse 1:8, He identifies Himself as, "the Lord God" (Adonay Yahveh), thereby referring to Himself as Sovereign Lord," as One Who is in total control of all that exists, which further means that no people or nation is ever beyond His absolute control!

Amos 1:9,10, God's prophesies His coming judgment against Tyre

It should be obvious by now that God is going from one neighboring nation to the next, around the nation of Israel, all of them her enemies, who sought to destroy her. And now at Amos 1:9,10, we see God prophesy His coming judgment against Tyre, as we there read, *"[9] Thus says the Lord, "For three transgressions of Tyre and for four I will not revoke its punishment, because they delivered up an entire population to Edom and did not remember the covenant of brotherhood. [10] So I will send fire upon the wall of Tyre and it will consume her citadels."*

Tyre was the principal trading port of the country of Phoenicia, just north of Israel on the Mediterranean Sea. Its merchant fleet traveled the known world. At Isaiah 23:3, Tyre is described as "the market of nations" and then at Isaiah 23:8, we read that her "traders were the honored of the earth."

And as we have seen from Joel 3:4-6, Tyre and Sidon (another city on the coast of Phoenicia) were involved with some of the cities of the Philistines in having "delivered an entire population to Edom," and as a result God was angry with them and here at verse 1:10 He promises to bring fire against them, which meant a complete destruction, for having been involved in taking people captive in Israel and then selling them in the slave markets of the world through Edom!

When God mentions "the covenant of the brotherhood" here at verse 1:9, He is most likely referring to the fact, as we see from 1 Kings 9:11, that Solomon had given Hiram, the king of Tyre, twenty cities in the region of Galilee, in the northern part of Israel, for having supplied him with all the cedar he needed when building his palace and the temple of The Lord in Jerusalem. And in this way, they shared the land of Israel, and so could be regarded as 'brothers.'

And so, as we see at verse 1:10, God prophesies a complete destruction as coming against the city of Tyre in the future, which the words, "I will send fire upon the wall of Tyre" indicates here! When God talks of "citadels," as He does here, and for a total of eleven times in His prophetic word through Amos, He is referring to a palace, if the place being mentioned is where the king resides, or else refers to fortified towers used for protection, as is the case here at verse 1:10.

Amos 1:11,12, God prophesies His judgment to come against Edom

As we then see from Amos 1:11,12, God now turns His gaze upon Edom and here prophesies of His coming judgment against them, as we there now read, *"[11] Thus says the Lord, "For three transgressions of Edom and for four I will not revoke its punishment, because he pursued his brother with the sword, while he stifled his compassion; his anger also tore continually, and he maintained his fury forever. [12] So I will send fire upon Teman and it will consume the citadels of Bozrah."*

We have already seen that Edom was involved in taking the captives that the Philistines and Phoenicians took from raids into the land of Israel and then sold them as slaves all over the world through the slave market of Edom, this having been something that God was going to severely judge those nations for. However, here at verse 1:11, God specifically focuses on the fact that Edom sought to destroy Israel at every turn, never showing any compassion, but only continual anger and fury in the carrying out of that goal!

God says of Edom here at verse 1:11, “he pursued his brother,” simply because Edom came from the descendants of Esau, who was Jacob’s twin brother! As such, he should have shown compassion, but did not, which should not surprise us for Esau was an unbeliever, while Jacob was a believer. Jacob was therefore serving God, while Esau was serving the devil, and God did prophesy at Genesis 3:15 that there would always be enmity between these two lines of descent!

And so, as we then see from verse 1:12 God’s judgment would be falling on Edom as a result, with two of its cities being mentioned here, namely Teman and Bozrah. Teman likely derives its name from the fact that Esau’s firstborn was Eliphaz, whose firstborn was Teman (1 Chronicles 1:35,36). Bozrah was a fortified city in northern Edom, which controlled access to the King’s Highway, by which caravans traveled through Edom. Let us note what God says at Isaiah 34:5 regarding Edom, “For My sword is satiated in heaven, behold it shall descend for judgment upon Edom and upon the people whom I have devoted to destruction. “

Amos 1:13-15, God prophesies His judgment to come against Ammon

God then turns His attention to Ammon, as another country surrounding Israel, and prophesies they too will experience His judgment, as we then see from Amos 1:13-15, *“[13] Thus says the Lord, "For three transgressions of the sons of Ammon and for four I will not revoke its punishment, because they ripped open the pregnant women of Gilead in order to enlarge their borders. [14] So I will kindle a fire on the wall of Rabbah and it will consume her citadels amid war cries on the day of battle, and a storm on the day of tempest. [15] Their king will go into exile, he and his princes together," says the Lord.”*

What we are to notice here is that Moab was just north of Edom and Ammon was just north of Moab. And like Edom, both Moab and Ammon derive from descendants of the sons of Israel, for as we see from Genesis 19:30-38, Lot, Abraham’s nephew, impregnated both his daughters while drunk, after the death of his wife. The one son born to them was named, “Moab” and the other “Ben-ammi,” who was the father of the sons of Ammon.

Then Gilead, mentioned at verse 1:13, was the territory to the north of Moab, which belonged to Israel after the conquest of this area by Moses at the time of their Exodus from Egypt. It was then given to the tribes of Reuben, Gad, and the half of Manasseh, as their inheritance in the land at the time of Joshua.

When we read here at verse 1:13 of what Ammon did in order to enlarge its territory, we have to realize that they were likely trying to regain the territory that once belonged to these two cousins, Moab and Ben-ammi. What angered God here was the way they went about it. When we read here, “they ripped open the pregnant women of Gilead,” we are to realize that God was likely giving a true description of what happened, in that they showed extreme cruelty, with no regard for human life! And that, just to enlarge its territory! And so, God pronounces His judgment to come against Ammon, mentioning Rabbah its capital here at verse 1:14, to indicate that the whole of the country was slated for a complete destruction, which would again be at the hands of the Assyrians.

As we then see at verse 1:15, when God’s judgment does fall, Ammon’s king and his sons will go into exile. Let us note what God says regarding Ammon at Jeremiah 49:2, “Therefore behold, the days are coming," declares the Lord, “That I will cause a trumpet blast of war to be heard against Rabbah of the sons of Ammon; and it will become a desolate heap, and her towns will be set on fire. Then Israel will take possession of his possessors," says the Lord,” and also at Ezekiel 25:4,5, “[4] therefore, behold, I am going to give you to the sons of the east for a possession, and they will set their encampments among you and make their dwellings among you; they will eat your fruit and drink your milk. [5] I will make Rabbah a pasture for camels and the sons of Ammon a resting place for flocks. Thus you will know that I am the Lord."

CHAPTER TWO

Amos 2:1-16

Amos 2:1-3, God prophesies His coming judgment against Moab

As God continues His prophetic word through Amos, we note from Amos 2:1-3 that he now pronounces His coming judgment against Moab, as we there read, *"[1] Thus says the Lord, "For three transgressions of Moab and for four I will not revoke its punishment, because he burned the bones of the king of Edom to lime. [2] So I will send fire upon Moab and it will consume the citadels of Kerioth; and Moab will die amid tumult, with war cries and the sound of a trumpet. [3] I will also cut off the judge from her midst and slay all her princes with him," says the Lord."*

Here we note that what God was specifically angry with Moab for was because they "burned the bones of the king of Edom to lime." The particular event that God has in view here is not found in Scripture. Nevertheless, we are to realize that God was displeased with this as He does not take lightly the desecration of a dead body, especially when it is done out of hatred for the person who has died. We need to remember here that Moab and Edom would be cousins, as we have seen, with Moab being a son of Lot, while Edom stood for Esau (noting Genesis 36:1,8), Jacob's brother.

Since we do not know the specifics of the event God has in mind here, then it is also possible that a human sacrifice to the god of Moab was involved here, possibly after winning a battle over the king of Edom, in which he would have been captured and then sacrificed to their god. If this was the case here, then we need to note what God says at Proverbs 21:27, "The sacrifice of the wicked is an abomination, how much more when he brings it with evil intent!" Whichever is the case here, God says that He will bring His judgment against Moab, for they have revealed their hearts to Him in what they have done, thereby showing themselves to be unbelievers!

At verse 2:2, God says that He will send His fire of judgment against "Kerioth," which was a city in Moab. Kerioth is mentioned three times in God's word and each time it is associated with God's judgment, here, and also at Jeremiah 48:21-24,40,41. When God says that He "will send fire upon Moab," He is indicating that a total destruction has been decreed! God's immediate judgment here would be coming at the hands of the Assyrians, although all subsequent invaders, such as the Babylonians, the Medes and Persians, and the Greeks, also brought a total devastation of the area!

It is interesting to see God cut off (that is, put to death), not only Moab's princes, to indicate no succession to the throne, but also mentions the cutting off of the judge from Moab, possibly because there was no Godly justice being meted out, such as in the matter of the burning to a lime the bones of the king of Edom.

Amos 2:4,5, God prophesies His judgment to come against the Southern kingdom of Judah

As we then see from Amos 2:4,5, after God had prophesied His judgment to come against the surrounding nations, He now turns His attention against the Southern kingdom of Judah here, as we now read, *"[4] Thus says the Lord, "For three transgressions of Judah and for four I will not revoke its punishment, because they rejected the law of the Lord and have not kept His statutes; their lies also have led them astray, those after which their fathers walked. [5] So I will send fire upon Judah and it will consume the citadels of Jerusalem."*

What we are to see here is that God had two primary reasons for raising the nation of Israel, starting with Abraham at Genesis 12 (the reader would benefit by reading Addendum C at this point). One primary reason for God raising up the nation of Israel was for God to have a nation of believers on earth, and through that one nation to spread the knowledge of Himself, and especially the knowledge of how to have a personal relationship with Himself through faith in His Son, and to spread that knowledge of salvation to all the other nations of the earth.

And so, early in Israel's history as a nation, God gave them HIS WRITTEN WORD, starting with Moses. During the time of Adam and his descendants in first age of time, man had been passing on the knowledge of God ORALLY; and now for the first time in history, we have God's word being transmitted in written form through the believers of the nation of Israel! Then the second primary reason for God raising up the nation of Israel was for the purpose OF BRINGING HIS SON TO EARTH, as He had promised to do at Genesis 3:15, which would be through believers of the nation of Israel.

However, what we are to also see here – and what should not be surprising, due to the fact that human beings do have a sinful nature inherited from our first father Adam – is that as the years progressed, the descendants of the believers that God used to first bring about the nation of Israel, namely Abraham, Isaac, Jacob and his twelve sons, started going astray from God, which led God to raise one PROPHET after another in order to bring the nation of Israel back to Himself, as is clear from what God tells us at Jeremiah 7:25,26, "[25] Since the day that your fathers came out of the land of Egypt until this day, I HAVE SENT YOU ALL MY SERVANTS THE PROPHETS, daily rising early and sending them. [26] YET YOU DID NOT LISTEN TO ME (that is, did not obey My word so as to carry it out) or incline their ear, but stiffened their neck; they did more evil than their fathers."

And so, coming back to Amos 2:4,5, God is now seen to be angry with the majority of those of the Southern kingdom of Judah, which consisted of the tribe of Judah and Benjamin, with its capital at Jerusalem, as where God chose to have His Name and His dwelling place on earth, by having His temple built there. And now we see that the people of Judah as a whole were not living in obedience to God's word, so as to carry it out on earth. This was a critical matter to God, because it was through the tribe of Judah that God's Son would be coming to earth one day, as born of a woman from that tribe (Micah 5:2).

Also, Judah was not fulfilling the reason for being raised of God, which was to transmit the knowledge of Himself to other nations. How were they going to accomplish this when they themselves were no longer living in accordance with God's word, but instead had turned to believing the devil's lies, who has been working since the time of Adam and Eve to prevent God's Son from coming to earth in human flesh! And so, God prophesies His coming judgment against Judah also, with that total destruction of the Southern kingdom of Judah and of the city of Jerusalem taking place later under the Babylonians, although the Assyrians did threaten them when bringing devastation to the surrounding nations, but God was protecting them, noting 2 Kings 19:32-36!

Amos 2:6-8, God prophesies His coming judgment against the Northern kingdom of Israel

Then at Amos 2:6-8, God turns His gaze on the Northern kingdom of Israel and prophesies that it too will undergo His judgment, noting now what we there read, *"[6] Thus says the Lord, "For three transgressions of Israel and for four I will not revoke its punishment, because they sell the righteous for money and the needy for a pair of sandals. [7] These who pant after the very dust of the earth on the head of the helpless also turn aside the way of the humble; and a man and his father resort to the same girl in order to profane My holy name. [8] On garments taken as pledges they stretch out beside every altar, and in the house of their God they drink the wine of those who have been fined."*

We notice here that God does not bring up any of the sins of the Southern kingdom of Judah, for He knows that the Northern kingdom of Israel has been in unbelief since its inception and as such will not obey Him, so as to live their lives in accordance with His will made known in His word. What we do see God point out here is their godless lifestyle, which was the result of their unbelief!

And so, instead of carrying out God's will, as made known in His word (as for instance Deuteronomy 15:7-11), those of the Northern kingdom of Israel were involved in practices that God was opposed to in His word. In other words, they practiced the very sins that God said in His word should not be done! They had no regard for those who showed themselves "righteous" among them, and they could not care less for the poor. They resorted to sexual sin that they knew was wrong, doing so just to thumb their nose at God. They even took the garments that were given as a pledge and used it as a mat to kneel on beside their idolatrous altars! And they even raised sacrificial cups of wine to idols that they had unjustly obtained through fines! In short, they not only dishonored and sinned against God, but also against their very own people! God was warning them here through Amos that they were now under His judgment for such sins, which we will see He also expands on later at Amos 5:12 and 8:6.

We should not regard the word "righteous" at verse 2:6 as meaning that these were believers among those of the Northern kingdom, as the word most often refers to. But rather here the word simply refers to those among them who tried to conform to an ethical or moral standard, such as at Isaiah 5:23, where we read, "Who justify the wicked for a bribe, and take away the rights of the ones who are in the right!" The term "who are in the right" is the same Hebrew word "Tsaddiq" as at Amos 2:6 for "righteous." It is important to be aware that when king Jeroboam introduced idolatry in the Northern kingdom of Israel, those who were righteous, that is, those who were believers through a personal relationship with God in salvation, all left the Northern kingdom of Israel and went to live in the Southern kingdom of Judah, noting 2 Chronicles 11:14,16!

Before we go further, it would be good for us to remember what God says to all believers at Romans 15:4, "For whatever was written in earlier times was written for our instruction, so that through perseverance and the encouragement of the Scriptures we might have hope," and also at 1 Corinthians 10:11, "Now these things happened to them as an example, and they were written for our instruction, upon whom the ends of the ages have come." What this means then is that we should not just be reading what we have read so far, and will yet further read regarding the nation of Israel, and say to ourselves, "Well, this does not apply to us now, but to those people to whom it was said." In other words, we cannot escape God's judgment either now if we commit the same sins as they did back then! God's warning then also applies to us now, in that He will judge all sin, which are always against Him (Psalm 51:4)!

Amos 2:9-16, God here reminds the nation of Israel as a whole what He did for them in the past, which should have rendered them to be in willing service to Him, but instead, they have turned from Him, and for this they can expect to be judged by Him!

As we then see from Amos 2:9-16, God now uses this occasion to remind the nation of Israel as a whole, that is, both the Southern kingdom of Judah and the Northern kingdom of Israel, what He has done for them since their beginning as a nation. For instead of willingly serving Him out of gratitude and love for Him, they have been weighing Him down with their sins, and for this, they can expect God's judgment, which is sure to come, noting now what we there read, *"[9] Yet it was I who destroyed the Amorite before them, though his height was like the height of cedars and he was strong as the oaks; I even destroyed his fruit above and his root below. [10] It was I who brought you up from the land of Egypt, and I led you in the wilderness forty years that you might take possession of the land of the Amorite. [11] Then I raised up some of your sons to be prophets and some of your young men to be Nazirites. Is this not so, O sons of Israel?" declares the Lord. [12] But you made the Nazirites drink wine, and you commanded the prophets saying, 'You shall not prophesy!' [13] Behold, I am weighted down beneath you as a wagon is weighted down when filled with sheaves. [14] Flight will perish from the swift, and the stalwart will not strengthen his power, nor the mighty man save his life. [15] He who grasps the bow will not stand his ground, the swift of foot will not escape, nor will he who rides the horse save his life. [16] Even the bravest among the warriors will flee naked in that day," declares the Lord."*

We are to note from verses 2:9,10 here that God calls the land of Canaan, that He gave to Israel as a possession, "the land of the Amorite," most likely because they were not only the larger number among the nations making up Canaan, but when the Exodus occurred under Moses, the Amorites were seen by the sons of Israel as tall as cedars and strong as oaks. God's point here is that of themselves the land they were now living in would never have become their possession, apart from God's intervention!

When God says at verse 2:10 here, “I even destroyed his fruit above and his root below,” He is here indicating that He has made an end to the Amorites, not only a nation, but also as a race, noting similar terminology to describe the same truth at Ezekiel 17:9 and Malachi 4:1.

God also reminds them here at verse 2:11,12 that He graciously raised some of their sons to be prophets, which was to speak to the people for God (noting Deuteronomy 18:18,19; Jeremiah 7:25,25) and to tell them of things to come; and also raised some of their sons as Nazirites, to be set apart for God’s use as holy to Him (Numbers 6:1-8). But again, instead of honoring God for His goodness to them, they asked the prophets not to speak to them in the Name of The Lord , and made the Nazirites drink wine to ruin their service to God!

And so, at verse 2:13 God says that because of their sins against Him, He feels like a wagon loaded down with sheaves at harvest time! And because this was so, God’s judgment will fall on them, as we see at verses 2:14-16, in that when God sends nations and kingdoms against them, such as the Assyrians and then later the Babylonians, then those who are swift will not be fast enough to escape; those who are strong will not find the strength to stand in battle; the mighty among them will likewise perish; those who hold the bow will likewise go down; those on horses will also be among the fallen; and even their best warriors will end up disarmed and defeated on the battlefield! In other words, once God has given them up to judgment, then there is no one that can escape or stand when that judgment comes! And so, God’s message to the nation of Israel here is as He says at Ezekiel 18:32, “For I have no pleasure in the death of anyone who dies," declares the Lord God. "Therefore, repent and live."”

CHAPTER THREE

Amos 3:1-15

Amos 3:1-8, God again prophesies through Amos that the nation of Israel will not escape God's judgment for all their sins against Him!

As God continues His prophetic word through Amos, we see from Amos 3:1-8 that He again addresses the nation of Israel as a whole, in letting them know that He will be judging their sins, as we there now read, *"[1] Hear this word which the Lord has spoken against you, sons of Israel, against the entire family which He brought up from the land of Egypt: [2] "You only have I chosen among all the families of the earth; therefore I will punish you for all your iniquities." [3] Do two men walk together unless they have made an appointment? [4] Does a lion roar in the forest when he has no prey? Does a young lion growl from his den unless he has captured something? [5] Does a bird fall into a trap on the ground when there is no bait in it? Does a trap spring up from the earth when it captures nothing at all? [6] If a trumpet is blown in a city will not the people tremble? If a calamity occurs in a city has not the Lord done it? [7] Surely the Lord God does nothing unless He reveals His secret counsel to His servants the prophets. [8] A lion has roared! Who will not fear? The Lord God has spoken! Who can but prophesy?"*

As we see from verse 3:1, God again addresses Himself to "the sons of Israel," whom He is threatening judgment against here, and adds that what He is saying is "against the entire family," meaning against the whole of the nation of Israel, which consisted at that time of both the Southern kingdom of Judah, consisting of the tribes of Judah and Benjamin, with its capital at Jerusalem, and to the Northern kingdom of Israel, consisting of the remaining ten tribes, with its capital at Samaria. For as God also mentions here at verse 3:1, it was all twelve tribes of Israel that God did bring up from Egypt at the time of their Exodus under Moses.

God then points out to the nation of Israel at verse 3:2 that they were a chosen nation, which God chose among all the nations of the earth. And as before indicated, which we need to keep in mind here, God chose the nation of Israel as a representative nation, so that whatever this nation does during its history, any other nation would likewise have done had it been chosen in Israel's place. Then secondly, God chose the nation of Israel to bring His word through them for all the other nations of the earth. And thirdly, God chose the nation of Israel to bring His Son to earth through! And so God says here, the fact that they are a chosen nation will not excuse them from being punished for their sin against Him!

Then as we see from verses 3:3-8, God then asks the nation of Israel a series of questions, which are rhetorical, that is, in which God is not looking for a verbal answer from them, but rather are designed to have them think about their current situation, in terms of whether they are walking with God by living in accordance with His word, and if they are not, then to make the needed correction!

And so, God's first rhetorical question at verse 3:3 is whether two men can walk together unless they have both agreed to do so? Let us note the interchange which took place at Exodus 19:5-8 between God, Moses, and the sons of Israel, as represented by their elders, as we there now read, "[5] 'Now then, if you will indeed obey My voice and keep My covenant, then you shall be My own possession among all the peoples, for all the earth is Mine; [6] and you shall be to Me a kingdom of priests and a holy nation.' These are the words that you shall speak to the sons of Israel." [7] So Moses came and called the elders of the people, and set before them all these words which the Lord had commanded him. [8] All the people answered together and said, "All that the Lord has spoken we will do!" And Moses brought back the words of the people to the Lord." And so, as we see from the above, Israel had indeed agreed to walk with God in the light of His word, and now they were no longer doing so!

Then God's second rhetorical question at verse 3:4, which is here stated two different ways, but both meaning the same thing, is whether a lion roars in triumph unless it has captured some prey? And so, just as a lion exists to catch prey in order to feed its family, so too does the nation of Israel exist to serve God, or else it has nothing to shout over, but rather should be ashamed!

Similarly at verse 3:5, God asks a third rhetorical question in which He uses two questions to basically say the same thing, namely that a bird does not get caught in a trap with no bait, while a trap does not spring unless there is something in the trap to spring for! The message to the nation of Israel here is that it was only going through the motions of serving God, which it was raised of God to do! They were giving Him lip service, but their hearts were far from Him!

God's fourth rhetorical question at verse 3:6 involves the blowing of a trumpet in a city, having here in mind the fact that a watchman over a city was to blow the trumpet to warn the residents therein that there was an enemy approaching and for them to be ready, noting Jeremiah 4:5,19; Ezekiel 33:2,3. God here says that such an event would make the people of the city tremble. So too then should the nation of Israel tremble, for it too has an enemy coming against it!

God then further asks a fifth rhetorical question at verse 3:6, namely if some calamity occurs in a city, was it not something that God allowed to happen? The message to the nation of Israel here is that the enemy that was coming against them was one that God Himself had raised against them, as an instrument in His Hand to bring His judgment to pass for all their sins against Him, noting Isaiah 14:24-27; 45:7!

Then at verses 3:7 God discloses that He does nothing without first announcing it in His word through a prophet that He has raised for this purpose (noting for example Genesis 6:13), which then leads Him to ask a sixth and seventh rhetorical question at verse 3:8, with both leading to the same conclusion. So God says here that a lion has roared, who will not fear, which meant, as God goes on to say, that He has spoken, which therefore means that His prophet, as here with Amos, has prophesied, which meant that the nation of Israel should now tremble at what God has said!

Amos 3:9-15, God here prophesies through Amos that the Northern kingdom of Israel should be aware of the coming total devastation at the hands of an enemy that was fast approaching!

As we then see from Amos 3:9-15, God now prophesies through Amos that an enemy was fast approaching, who will bring total devastation to the Northern kingdom of Israel as a judgment for all her sins, noting now what we there read, *"[9] Proclaim on the citadels in Ashdod and on the citadels in the land of Egypt and say, "Assemble yourselves on the mountains of Samaria and see the great tumults within her and the oppressions in her midst. [10] But they do not know how to do what is right," declares the Lord, "these who hoard up violence and devastation in their citadels." [11] Therefore, thus says the Lord God, "An enemy, even one surrounding the land, will pull down your strength from you and your citadels will be looted." [12] Thus says the Lord, "Just as the shepherd snatches from the lion's mouth a couple of legs or a piece of an ear, so will the sons of Israel dwelling in Samaria be snatched away — with the corner of a bed and the cover of a couch! [13] Hear and testify against the house of Jacob," declares the Lord God, the God of hosts. [14] For on the day that I punish Israel's transgressions, I will also punish the altars of Bethel; the horns of the altar will be cut off and they will fall to the ground. [15] I will also smite the winter house together with the summer house; the houses of ivory will also perish and the great houses will come to an end," declares the Lord."*

At verse 3:9 here, God calls on the those in the fortified towers of Ashdod and Egypt to come to the mountains of Samaria, which is here representing the whole of the Northern kingdom of Israel, and for them to be observers of the chaos and confusion that will be taking place there, due to the presence of enemy oppressors who will be coming among them, which would be Assyria here!

At verse 3:10, God explains that this calamity would be occurring due to those of the Northern kingdom of Israel not living in accordance with God's word, and as a result have stored for themselves the cruelty and devastation that an enemy would soon be inflicting upon them! As we then see from verse 3:11, God says that this enemy now surrounding the land will remove from them all that they are relying upon in this world and will be looting their fortified towers, where their supplies against a siege would be stored!

Then at verse 3:12, God likens what happens when a lion attacks a sheep to illustrate what will happen when the enemy, Assyria, comes and snatches the inhabitants of the Northern kingdom of Israel and takes them into exile, with God at verses 3:13 calling on those who hear God's word, such as Amos, to testify as to the truth of what God has said here regarding the Northern kingdom of Israel.

God then declares at verses 3:14,15 that when His devastation of the Northern kingdom of Israel comes, which will be at the hands of the Assyrians (noting 2 Kings 17:6), He will start by first of all causing a complete destruction of the idolatrous altar at Bethel that Jeroboam, king of Israel, had caused to be erected there (noting 1 Kings 12:25-33; Hosea 10:5-8,14,15) and which had become a source of sinful pride and defiance; then He will go on to have the king's summer and winter residences looted and destroyed; and then will go on and have all the houses of importance looted and devastated also, so that the Northern kingdom of Israel will be left in total ruin!

CHAPTER FOUR

Amos 4:1-13

Amos 4:1-3, God here prophesies that the leadership of the Northern kingdom of Israel, which was at Samaria, its capital, was about to be carried away into exile!

As God continues His prophetic word through Amos, we see from Amos 4:1-3 that He now prophesies that the leadership of the Northern kingdom of Israel, which was at Samaria, its capital, was about to be carried away into exile, noting what we there now read, *"[1] Hear this word, you cows of Bashan who are on the mountain of Samaria, who oppress the poor, who crush the needy, who say to your husbands, "Bring now, that we may drink!" [2] The Lord God has sworn by His holiness, "Behold, the days are coming upon you when they will take you away with meat hooks, and the last of you with fish hooks. [3] You will go out through breaches in the walls, each one straight before her, and you will be cast to Harmon," declares the Lord."*

It is important to grasp that God is here speaking to the leadership of the Northern kingdom of Israel, which was at its capital, Samaria, which God has in view when saying "the mountain of Samaria." The word "mountain" is singular here and therefore refers to the city of Samaria, which had been built on a hilltop. The same is true again at Amos 6:1. However, at Amos 3:9, when God spoke of "the mountains of Samaria," He was there speaking of the Northern kingdom of Israel as a whole, which was often also referred to as 'Samaria.'

Then we further need to be aware that God uses a metaphor here in calling the leadership of the Northern kingdom of Israel "you cows of Bashan." For just as cows (heifers) are often rebellious, the leadership of the Northern kingdom of Israel at Samaria was likewise rebellious against God, in that they were not living and acting in accordance with God's word, for they were exploiting the poor and ill-treating the needy, which was contrary to what God wanted to see!

The phrase here, "who say to your husbands, "Bring now that we may drink!,"" is here a reference to "the needy," who were just in view. Therefore, the word rendered "husbands" at verse 4:1 would be better rendered 'their lords,' which is the literal rendering of the word "husbands" here!

It is clear from verse 4:2,3 that God's judgment was near for the Northern kingdom of Israel, with God here using very descriptive language to depict their impending exile to Assyria as not only being terrifying, but also very deadly! It is not too often we see God swear by His Holiness, which means that this will occur for sure! The mention of meat hooks and fish hooks give a picture here of extreme pain that will be accompanying their exile. In other words, it will not take place on plush cushions in horse-drawn carriages!

The mention of their being "cast to Harmon" is hard to determine as to its precise meaning, since the word "Harmon" only occurs here in Scripture. Since God says, "you will be cast," which is a term He uses at Luke 12:5 to describe those He will one day cast into hell, then the meaning here may be that their dead bodies will be cast to the garbage heap, since the mention of meat hooks and fish hooks give us a picture of what would remain of a human body would be a corpse! The mention of going "through breaches in the wall" is a reference to those trying to escape through the siege wall around Samaria, that the Assyrians will build when they come to take them into exile!

Amos 4:4,5, God here declares why Samaria will be exiled!

As we then see from Amos 4:4,5, God now gives some reasons why the Northern kingdom of Israel will be exiled, noting what we there read, *"[4] Enter Bethel and transgress; in Gilgal multiply transgression! Bring your sacrifices every morning, your tithes every three days. [5] Offer a thank offering also from that which is leavened, and proclaim freewill offerings, make them known. For so you love to do, you sons of Israel," declares the Lord God."*

God mentions Bethel here because this was the main place of worship for those of the Northern kingdom of Israel, which had been set up as a place of idol worship through king Jeroboam, which meant that everything that was done there was but a transgression against God! Then God also mentions Gilgal, as where the worship of God was taking place when the nation of Israel first entered the land of Canaan under Joshua (Joshua 5:10; 1 Samuel 11:14,15), and where much sin was taking place, noting here for instance what God said through the prophet Hosea at verse 9:15, "All their evil is at Gilgal; indeed, I came to hate them there! Because of the wickedness of their deeds I will drive them out of My house! I will love them no more; all their princes are rebels"

And so, since much sin was taking place in the worship of God by those of the Northern kingdom of Israel, God then goes on at verse 4:5 and tells those of the Northern kingdom of Israel that they might as well also bring their daily sacrifices and their tithe while they are in the process of sinning against Him! In other words, worship of God was to be with praise and thanksgiving out of a pure heart filled with love for Him. Since this was not the case for them, then they might as well go all the way in their sinful attempt at worship! "sin good"

God gives some examples of their sinful worship at verse 4:5, when He there mentions their thank offering, which was part of the 'peace offering,' and was supposed to be made to offer God thanks for blessings received, was being made with leaven, which was a picture of the presence of sin, noting Leviticus 2:11; 12:11,12. It was supposed to be made in such a way as to be accepted by God (Leviticus 22:29). But they not only made their thank offering with leaven, but they also boasted about their freewill offerings to God, which were supposed to be a matter between themselves and God, and not become one of sinful pride! And so, this kind of worship was not acceptable to God, and for this they would be judged by Him!

Amos 4:6-13, God here describes to Samaria all that He has done by way of judgment, in order to prevent their being exiled, but they refused to return to Him!

God is a God of mercy, and it is never His desire to see anyone perish (Ezekiel 18:23,32). Those who perish do so of their own freewill. And so, God always offers human beings opportunities to turn from one's sin and to be in right relationship with Him. This is what we see God do here at Amos 4:6-13, as He describes for the Northern kingdom of Israel all that He has done for them in judgment, to prevent their being exiled, but unfortunately they still were not listening to Him, so as to prevent it from taking place, noting now what we there read, *"[6] But I gave you also cleanness of teeth in all your cities and lack of bread in all your places, yet you have not returned to Me," declares the Lord. [7] Furthermore, I withheld the rain from you while there were still three months until harvest. Then I would send rain on one city and on another city I would not send rain; one part would be rained on, while the part not rained on would dry up. [8] So two or three cities would stagger to another city to drink water, but would not be satisfied; yet you have not returned to Me," declares the Lord. [9] I smote you with scorching wind and mildew; and the caterpillar was devouring your many gardens and vineyards, fig trees and olive trees; yet you have not returned to Me," declares the Lord. [10] I sent a plague among you after the manner of Egypt; I slew your young men by the sword along with your captured horses, and I made the stench of your camp rise up in your nostrils; yet you have not returned to Me," declares the Lord. 11] I overthrew you, as God overthrew Sodom and Gomorrah, and you were like a firebrand snatched from a blaze; yet you have not returned to Me," declares the Lord. [12] Therefore thus I will do to you, O Israel; because I will do this to you, prepare to meet your God, O Israel." [13] For behold, He who forms mountains and creates the wind and declares to man what are His thoughts, He who makes dawn into darkness and treads on the high places of the earth, The Lord God of hosts is His name."*

The reference to those of the Northern kingdom of Israel having "cleanness of teeth" at verse 4:6 here meant that God, in judgment against them, had withheld blessing their crop yield, which meant that they did not have much to eat, which is further seen as they then were lacking bread o eat in all their dwellings. In God's book of Judges, when the people of Israel experienced hardship through God allowing their enemies to bring them into bondage, they turned to God and cried to Him for help, which He provided time and time again (noting for instance Judges 2:7-15). However, here those of the Northern kingdom of Israel were NOT turning to God in order to likewise experience His Hand of deliverance, which showed that they had become hardened by sin!

Then at verse 4:7,8, we further see what God did in judgment to get them to turn to Him, such as withholding the rain, or else sending rain in only one location, but even then there never was enough. This meant that they did not have the required rain for a bountiful harvest. And again, even though those of the Northern kingdom of Israel would have noticed that God's blessing had been removed from them, they still did not turn to Him for relief from His Hand of judgment!

Then again at verse 4:9, God points out that He even sent a scorching wind, mildew, and caterpillars to ruin their crops, in order to let them know that His Hand of blessing had been removed from them, and to show that they were under His judgment, and even then, they did not turn to Him, showing just how hardened their sinful hearts had become!

Then again at verse 4:10, God says that He even sent a plague among them, as He had done in Egypt at that time of Moses; and even allowed their young men to fall in battle, along with the horses taken as spoil, so that the stench in their camp rose up in their nostrils, and even then they did not take heed to God's Hand of judgment, and they still refused to turn to Him!

As we then see at verse 4:11, when their enemies came against them, God allowed them to be overthrown, although He still maintained some of them alive, and even then they still would not see the light and turn from the darkness of sin to God, to receive relief from His Hand of judgment!

And so, as we then see at verses 4:12, those of the Northern kingdom of Israel have not left God any choice, and so He tells them here to prepare to meet their God, with His then describing Himself at verse 4:13, as being The God with Whom they will have to do! Then for added emphasis, in terms of them needing to fear The God they would now be coming in contact with in judgment, God now describes Himself as The One Who caused the mountains to exist; Who brings forth the wind by His command; Who can read the mind of any human being and reveal one's thoughts; Who makes even the highest mountains of the earth as stepping stones for His feet! His Name is "The Lord God of hosts!" As we have seen at verse 1:8, He there identified Himself as, "the Lord God" (Adonay Yahveh), thereby referring to Himself as "Sovereign Lord," as One Who is in total control of all that exists, which further means that no people or nation is ever beyond His absolute control!

It is also important to be aware here that when God calls Himself, "the Lord God of hosts," He is referring to Himself as not only Sovereign over all that exists, but also as Commander-In-Chief of all the armies of Heaven and also of the nation of Israel on earth. We need to note that when Joshua had been appointed to lead Israel in battle to conquer the land of Canaan, God's Son appeared to him in a Christophany (a preIncarnate temporary appearance on earth), as we see at Joshua 5:13,14, "[13] Now it came about when Joshua was by Jericho, that he lifted up his eyes and looked, and behold, a man was standing opposite him with his sword drawn in his hand, and Joshua went to him and said to him, "Are you for us or for our adversaries?" [14] He said, "No; rather I indeed come now as CAPTAIN OF THE HOST (same word) OF THE LORD." And Joshua fell on his face to the earth, and bowed down, and said to him, "What has my lord to say to his servant?"" And this was now The God they would have to answer to!

CHAPTER FIVE

Amos 5:1-27

Amos 5:1-7, God here calls on the Northern kingdom of Israel to seek Him and live!

As God continues His prophetic word through Amos, He now calls on the Northern kingdom of Israel, as we see at Amos 5:1-7, to seek Him in order to go on living, noting what we there now read, *"[1] Hear this word which I take up for you as a dirge, O house of Israel: [2] She has fallen, she will not rise again — The virgin Israel. She lies neglected on her land; there is none to raise her up. [3] For thus says the Lord God, "The city which goes forth a thousand strong will have a hundred left, and the one which goes forth a hundred strong will have ten left to the house of Israel." [4] For thus says the Lord to the house of Israel, "Seek Me that you may live. [5] But do not resort to Bethel and do not come to Gilgal, nor cross over to Beersheba; for Gilgal will certainly go into captivity and Bethel will come to trouble. [6] Seek the Lord that you may live, or He will break forth like a fire, O house of Joseph, and it will consume with none to quench it for Bethel, [7] for those who turn justice into wormwood and cast righteousness down to the earth.""*

We see God say to the Northern kingdom of Israel at verse 5:1,2 that He has a word for them, which He will give to them as a dirge, which was, "She has fallen, she will not rise again." A dirge was a lament for the dead that one made at a funeral. And so, God's prophetic message to the Northern kingdom of Israel here is that they will fall and there will be no one to help them when that happens!

At verse 5:3, in order to amplify what He has just said, God now tells the Northern kingdom of Israel that when His judgment falls, in terms of allowing Assyria to come and devastate their land and bring them into exile, the city that now has a thousand strong will be reduced to a hundred, and the city that has a hundred strong will be reduced to ten! In light of this, God calls on them at verse 5:4 to seek Him before it is too late, so that they might go on living!

Then we see God say at verse 5:5-7 to the Northern kingdom of Israel, whom God refers to as "the house of Israel" and also "the house of Joseph," that there is no point in their trying to find refuge at Bethel or at Gilgal, for the one will come to nothing and the other will go into exile; nor were they even to cross over to the town of Beersheba in the remotest southern part of the Southern kingdom of Judah, in their attempt to escape God's judgment, for the remedy was not in escaping, but rather in turning to God in order to live! God was about to come to them in the fire of judgment, with none to quench it, for they were at present ripe for judgment due to turning justice into wormwood, that is, as what was bitter and unpleasant for those on the receiving end, and intent on not doing what was right in the eyes of God, thereby extinguishing His righteousness from their midst!

Amos 5:8,9, God again takes a moment to declare Who He is, as The One they will be facing in judgment!

God now takes a moment to again declare to the Northern kingdom of Israel, Who He is, as God had done earlier at verse 4:13, since He is The One they will be facing in judgment, noting what we now here read, *"[8] He who made the Pleiades and Orion and changes deep darkness into morning, who also darkens day into night, who calls for the waters of the sea and pours them out on the surface of the earth, the Lord is His name. [9] It is He who flashes forth with destruction upon the strong, so that destruction comes upon the fortress."*

At verse 5:8, God wants those of the Northern kingdom of Israel in unbelief to look up at the sky and there see "the Pleiades," that is, a cluster of stars visible with the naked eye, and also "Orion," which was another fixed group of stars visible to the naked eye, which appeared in the form of a person, with God pointing out here that He was The One Who had made these!

And not only that, but He was also The One turning the darkness of night into the light of morning and the light of day into the darkness of night again. In other words, this physical phenomena was also what was under His Divine control, just as was the water cycle, that had the wind pass over the seas to collect the moisture into clouds and then bring these over land, so as to water the land for the benefit of God's creation! God here says that it is The Lord, Who does this, that is His Name!

As we then see at verse 5:9, God now drives the point home to the Northern kingdom of Israel that since He can do these extraordinary things in the physical world, then they can be sure that it is as nothing for Him to defeat even the strongest foe and destroy even the most fortified fortress! Let us note what God says at Isaiah 29:5, "But the multitude of your enemies will become like fine dust, and the multitude of the ruthless ones like the chaff which blows away; and it will happen instantly, suddenly." This was therefore The God they had to do with!

Amos 5:10-15, after again naming some of the sins of those of the Northern kingdom of Israel, God again seeks to have them turn to Him from their evil ways!

One of many things that is heartwarming about God is that He does not give up on His human creation! We see this again here at verses 5:10-15, for after again pointing out some of the sinful things that those of the Northern kingdom of Israel were doing, God again seeks to turn them to Himself from their evil ways, as we there now read, *"[10] They hate him who reproves in the gate, and they abhor him who speaks with integrity. [11] Therefore because you impose heavy rent on the poor and exact a tribute of grain from them, though you have built houses of well-hewn stone, yet you will not live in them; you have planted pleasant vineyards, yet you will not drink their wine. [12] For I know your transgressions are many and your sins are great, you who distress the righteous and accept bribes and turn aside the poor in the gate. [13] Therefore at such a time the prudent person keeps silent, for it is an evil time. [14] Seek good and not evil, that you may live; And thus may the Lord God of hosts be with you, just as you have said! [15] Hate evil, love good, and establish justice in the gate! Perhaps the Lord God of hosts may be gracious to the remnant of Joseph."*

We are to see that when God speaks of the "gate" in this passage (verses 5:10,12,15), He is referring to the main square of a town or city, where the king sat, if it was a royal city (noting 2 Samuel 19:8), or where the elders sat, if it was not, and there would make decisions for all those who came to them with a problem or issue that needed a solution (noting Deuteronomy 22:15; 25:7; Ruth 4:1-6).

And so we see from verse 5:10,11 that those of the Northern kingdom of Israel hated those who dared point out things that were wrong among them, and detested those who spoke with a moral compass. They imposed a high rent to the poor living on their land and exacted an obligation of grain from them, which meant that they showed themselves heartless to those who were in greatest need among them!

As a result, God points out in the rest of verse 5:11 that He sees and will judge such sins, for those who have well-built homes will not continue to live in them, and those who have productive vineyards will not be drinking the wine derived from it, for they are about to go into exile!

Unfortunately, as we see from verse 5:12, this was not the full extent of the sins they were committing, for as God further points out here, they were not leaving alone those among them who tried to live their lives in accordance to some moral compass, but rather kept troubling them, and they also accepted bribes from the rich, while not lifting a finger to help the poor, who sought help from those who were in a position to provide it! As God says at verse 5:13, in such an evil time as this, those who still exercised good judgment among them were laying low and not making things worse for themselves by speaking up! As God says at Ecclesiastes 3:7, they knew the time to speak and also the time to remain silent!

Then we again see God reach out to those of the Northern kingdom of Israel at verse 5:14, letting them know that devastation of their land and exile need not be their lot, if they would only seek to do good, instead of the evil they were doing. God would then turn from His prophesied coming judgment upon them and would again be with them, as they knew He had been in the past, and as some were still claiming He was. For as God says at verse 5:15, all they had to do was to hate evil and love good, which was the reverse of what they were now doing, while carrying out true justice at the gate, instead of taking advantage of their fellowman for their own benefit! If they did this, then God would see and would respond in kind on all among them who were willing to turn to Him.

It is important to see from Genesis 18:22-33 that Abraham was interceding with God on behalf of Sodom and Gomorrah, and there we see that even though God was planning to destroy these cities, nevertheless He would refrain from doing so if He found ten who were righteous there! And so, we see that God was looking for at least ten here in the Northern kingdom of Israel to turn from sin to Him at this time, for Him to extend His mercy on the whole!

Amos 5:16,17, God here prophesies that the time that is coming will be a time of sorrow and mourning!

When God's judgment does come on the Northern kingdom it will not be that God had not warned them in advance as to what would occur, as is clear here again from what God prophesies at Amos 5:16,17, where He plainly tells them that a time of sorrow and mourning is coming upon the land, noting what we there now read, *"[16] Therefore thus says the Lord God of hosts, the Lord, "There is wailing in all the plazas, and in all the streets they say, 'Alas! Alas!' They also call the farmer to mourning and professional mourners to lamentation. [17] And in all the vineyards there is wailing, because I will pass through the midst of you," says the Lord."*

As we see from verses 5:16,17 here, God here paints a picture of what it would soon take place and what it would be like when God visits them in His judgment, by sending Assyria against them. People in all walks of life will be crying and mourning everywhere one looks. It is noteworthy here that God refers to Himself as, "the Lord God of hosts, the Lord," that is, as The Lord God, Head of armies, The Almighty!

Amos 5:18-20, God asks why some were longing for the day of the Lord?

It was obvious from what we now see God say at Amos 5:18-20 that those who were longing for 'the day of the Lord' did not know what they were longing for, as is clear from what we there read, *"[18] Alas, you who are longing for the day of the Lord, for what purpose will the day of the Lord be to you? It will be darkness and not light; [19] as when a man flees from a lion and a bear meets him, or goes home, leans his hand against the wall and a snake bites him. [20] Will not the day of the Lord be darkness instead of light, even gloom with no brightness in it?"*

It seems that some of the Northern kingdom of Israel thought that "the day of the Lord" meant a time other than what it actually would turn out to be. And so, in order to remove any misunderstanding, so that no one is caught by surprise when "the day of the Lord" actually comes, God now plainly says at verse 5:18 that this day will be a time of God's judgment, so that it will be a dark time in every way, physically, spiritually, emotionally, and mentally!

It is also clear from God's illustrations of that day at verse 5:19, that it will not be a pleasant experience, as what one would choose to have happen, such as to escape a lion, only to be caught by a bear, or to innocently lean against a wall and have a snake bite one's hand! And so God concludes by saying at verse 5:20 that the coming day of The Lord will be a time of gloom and doom, not a time of for joy and gladness!

Amos 5:21-24, God here lets the Northern kingdom of Israel know what He hated about their present practices, and what He wanted to see instead!

As we again see from Amos 5:21-24, God never brings His judgment upon any human being without first pointing out what one was doing wrong and what He would like to see instead, and this is now the case in regards to the Northern kingdom of Israel, as we there now read, *"[21] I hate, I reject your festivals, nor do I delight in your solemn assemblies. [22] Even though you offer up to Me burnt offerings and your grain offerings, I will not accept them; and I will not even look at the peace offerings of your fatlings. [23] Take away from Me the noise of your songs; I will not even listen to the sound of your harps.[24] But let justice roll down like waters and righteousness like an ever-flowing stream."*

The practices that God hated, as we see from verses 5:21-23, but which the Northern kingdom of Israel was persisting in, was worship which was ritualistic and not from the heart! They observed the feast days and solemn assemblies that God called for in His word, even offering the prescribed animal sacrifices and offerings with singing; however, none of this was done out of love for God, for what He would do for them in the future in sending His Son to earth to die in the place of a sinful human race, which the animal sacrifices and offerings were all intended to picture! Since they were in unbelief, their eyes and hearts were darkened as to the meaning of what they were observing and of what they were singing! And as a result, as we see here, God did not want any part of it!

All He wanted from them, as we see from verse 5:24, was for them to do justice, which would not happen until they lived their lives in accordance with God's word, and to also live righteously, which would not happen until they had received God's eternal life, which would be theirs once they had turned to Him by faith in His coming Son to receive the forgiveness of their sins!

Amos 5:25-27, God reminds the Northern kingdom of Israel that their waywardness had been with them since the time they left Egypt, and for that they will not escape their coming exile!

As God then reminds the Northern kingdom of Israel at verses 5:25-27, their waywardness had been part of their daily life even from the time they left Egypt, and for that they will not escape their coming exile, as we there now see, *"[25] Did you present Me with sacrifices and grain offerings in the wilderness for forty years, O house of Israel? [26] You also carried along Sikkuth your king and Kiyyun, your images, the star of your gods which you made for yourselves. [27] Therefore, I will make you go into exile beyond Damascus," says the Lord, whose name is the God of hosts."*

God's point here at verses 5;25,26 is that those of the Northern kingdom of Israel were part of those who from the time of their departure from Egypt had always been unbelievers, which was shown by the fact that when Moses led them out of Egypt, they brought with them the gods that they had been worshipping during their 430 year sojourn in Egypt!

Let us note as examples here what God had said back at Deuteronomy 32:17 in this regard, “They sacrificed to demons who were not God, to gods whom they have not known, new gods who came lately, whom your fathers did not dread,” and also at Joshua 24:14, “Now, therefore, fear the Lord and serve Him in sincerity and truth; and put away the gods which your fathers served beyond the River and in Egypt, and serve the Lord.” The reality here is that when one refuses to serve God, due to refusing to believe in Him for salvation, then one will serve gods of one’s choosing, even the devil. And so, as a result, they will not escape being exiled “beyond Damascus” in Syria, for they would be on their way to the territory under Assyria’s control.

What would also be instructive here is noting how God interprets verse 5:25-27 later at Acts 7:42,43, when there recounting Israel’s past history, there reading, “[42] But God turned away and delivered them up to serve the host of heaven; as it is written in the book of the prophets (that is, Amos), 'It was not to Me that you offered victims and sacrifices forty years in the wilderness, was it, O house of Israel? [43] You also took along the tabernacle of Moloch and the star of the god Rompha, the images which you made to worship. I also will remove you beyond Babylon.'

CHAPTER SIX

Amos 6:1-14

Amos 6:1-3, God pronounces a woe on both the Southern kingdom of Judah and on the Northern kingdom of Israel, letting them know that they were not any better than other kingdoms of this world!

As God continues His prophetic word through Amos, we now see Him pronounce a woe on both the Southern kingdom of Judah and the Northern kingdom of Israel, letting them know at Amos 6:1-3 that they were not any better than any other kingdom of this world, noting now what we there read, *"[1] Woe to those who are at ease in Zion and to those who feel secure in the mountain of Samaria, the distinguished men of the foremost of nations, to whom the house of Israel comes. [2] Go over to Calneh and look, and go from there to Hamath the great, then go down to Gath of the Philistines. are they better than these kingdoms, or is their territory greater than yours? [3] Do you put off the day of calamity, and would you bring near the seat of violence?"*

It is important to see that when God pronounces a woe against "Zion" at verse 6:1 here, it is against the city of Jerusalem, as the capital of the Southern kingdom of Judah, and when doing so against "the mountain of Samaria," God is addressing the city of Samaria, which was the capital of the Northern kingdom of Israel, which sat on a hilltop.

And when God refers to them as "the distinguished men of the foremost of nations," also at verse 6:1, it was by way of derision, as to laugh at the thought of them being so prideful, and thinking themselves better than other kingdoms! To prove His point, God calls on them, as we see at verse 6:2 to visit these other kingdoms, such as the city-state of Calneh and Hamath in Aram, and Gath in the territory of the Philistines, which had all once been prominent in the world, but now had been devastated and brought to ruin. So God asks them at the end of verse 6:2 if they think that they themselves really think that they will escape the same fate?

And so, as we then see at verse 6:3, God asks them, by inference, if they thought that in the way they were presently living, which was ungodly, they really thought that they could postpone their coming day of calamity and the reign of terror that was fast approaching!

Amos 6:4-7, God now specifically focuses on those in a position of power in the Northern kingdom of Israel, namely its kings, who therefore had the power to lead the nation in a Godly way, and did not, these will be at the head of those going into exile!

As we then see from Amos 6:4-7, God was certainly not finished, as He now focuses on those in a position of power in the Northern kingdom of Israel, namely its kings, who therefore had the power to lead the nation in a Godly way, but did not, these will be at the head of those going into exile, as we now there read, *"[4] Those who recline on beds of ivory and sprawl on their couches, and eat lambs from the flock and calves from the midst of the stall, [5] who improvise to the sound of the harp, and like David have composed songs for themselves, [6] who drink wine from sacrificial bowls while they anoint themselves with the finest of oils, yet they have not grieved over the ruin of Joseph. [7] Therefore, they will now go into exile at the head of the exiles, and the sprawlers' banqueting will pass away."*

It is important to see that God is being righteously critical of the kings of the Northern kingdom of Israel here, in what He is describing at verses 6:4-7, since they not only spent their days in luxury, but also in banqueting and entertainment, while not being concerned for the spiritual welfare of the those they were leading! When God speaks of their not being "grieved over the ruin of Joseph," He is alluding to the fact that people under their leadership were going to a lost eternity, while they lived only for this world. The mention of drinking wine from "sacrificial bowls" at verse 6:6, which were literally 'sprinkling basins,' was simply to emphasize that they had much to excess of what they wanted at the expense of the people. ,For all that, God says they will be at the head of those going into exile!

Amos 6:8-11, God here prophesies that He will raise up an enemy against the Northern kingdom of Israel, because He hates its arrogance of relying on their fortified towers, rather than relying on Him!

As we then see from Amos 6:8-11, God prophesies through Amos that He will raise up an enemy against the Northern kingdom of Israel, because He hates their arrogance in relying on its fortified towers, rather than relying on God, as we there now read, *"[8] The Lord God has sworn by Himself, the Lord God of hosts has declared: "I loathe the arrogance of Jacob, and detest his citadels; therefore I will deliver up the city and all it contains." [9] And it will be, if ten men are left in one house, they will die. [10] Then one's uncle, or his undertaker, will lift him up to carry out his bones from the house, and he will say to the one who is in the innermost part of the house, "Is anyone else with you?" And that one will say, "No one." Then he will answer, "Keep quiet. For the name of the Lord is not to be mentioned." [11] For behold, the Lord is going to command that the great house be smashed to pieces and the small house to fragments."*

When God swears by Himself, on His own authority and power, as we see Him do at verse 6:8, then this means that the Northern kingdom of Israel has been consigned to exile, here represented by "the city," which is its capital, Samaria. The matter has now been sealed and is irrevocable, due to the fact that instead of turning to God and living by His word, carrying out His will, they were relying on their own earthly resources, such as their fortified towers throughout the land.

God then describes at verses 6:9-11 what will soon be taking place throughout the Northern kingdom of Israel, in that not only will there be corpses everywhere, with no place to hide, but there will also be a total devastation coming, from the king's palace down to the homes of the ordinary person!

The mention at the end of verse 6:10, "Then he will answer, "Keep quiet. For the name of the Lord is not to be mentioned,"" relates to the fact that since God is The One Who will have brought this calamity to the Northern kingdom of Israel as part of His judgment for their rejection of Him, then if one is found alive during that time of judgment, it would be advisable to not mention the Name of The Lord for fear that God might hear that there is still someone alive and come and have him killed! In other words, God is giving those of the Northern kingdom of Israel here a picture of just how afraid those in unbelief will be of God when His time of judgment does come!

Amos 6:12-14, God asks some rhetorical questions of those of the Northern kingdom of Israel, which were nonsensical, in order to point out to them that the way they were living was not only sinful, but also nonsensical!

As God continues at Amos 6:12-14, He now asks the Northern kingdom of Israel some rhetorical questions, which were nonsensical in order to point out to them that the way they were living was not only sinful, but also nonsensical, noting now what we there read, *"[12] Do horses run on rocks? Or does one plow them with oxen? Yet you have turned justice into poison and the fruit of righteousness into wormwood, [13] you who rejoice in Lodebar, and say, "Have we not by our own strength taken Karnaim for ourselves?" [14] For behold, I am going to raise up a nation against you, O house of Israel," declares the Lord God of hosts, "and they will afflict you from the entrance of Hamath to the brook of the Arabah.""*

As we see starting at verse 6:12, God asks those of the Northern kingdom of Israel some rhetorical questions, such as, 'have you ever seen horses run on rocks?' and 'do you plow over rocks with your oxen?,' which would be answered as, 'certainly not!.' Here we see God ask these questions only to make them realize that while such things as He mentioned were nonsensical to them, yet God also sees them do things which were nonsensical to Him, such perverting justice, so that those searching for it found themselves the worse for it! And they also turned the fruit of righteousness into bitterness for those they came in contact with, instead of the beneficial effect that God wanted to see from their lives.

God again derides their folly at verse 6:13 by saying to them that they were apt to rejoice at things, which were in fact nothing, which the word "Lodebar" literally means here, when they claimed to have taken a place of no consequence called, "Karnaim," by their own strength, which word literally meant, 'a pair of horns.' In other words, they were taking pride in what was in fact nothing at all, which again showed the emptiness of the ungodly way of life!

And so, as we then see at verse 6:14, God says that He will raise up a nation against them, which would be Assyria, and they will end up being afflicted at the time of their exile, all the way from one end of their own country, from "the brook of Arabah" to the other end, at "the entrance of Hamath!"

CHAPTER SEVEN

Amos 7:1-17

Amos 7:1-3, God gives Amos a vision of calamity being planned, as a warning to the Northern kingdom of Israel!

As God continues His prophetic word through Amos, we now see from Amos 7:1-3 that He gives the prophet Amos a vision of calamity planned by God, as we there now read, *"[1] Thus the Lord God showed me, and behold, He was forming a locust-swarm when the spring crop began to sprout. And behold, the spring crop was after the king's mowing. [2] And it came about, when it had finished eating the vegetation of the land, that I said, "Lord God, please pardon! How can Jacob stand, for he is small?" [3] The Lord changed His mind about this. "It shall not be," said the Lord."*

It is important to see here that God gives a vision to Amos of WHAT HE COULD DO, IF HE WANTED TO, AS A WARNING to the Northern kingdom of Israel ! And so, in this vision, Amos was allowed of God to see at verse 7:1 a swarm of locust coming on the second crop of the year, just after the first crop had been harvested, which crop had been for the king and his household, while that second crop was for the people themselves, which meant there would be scarcity if that swarm of locusts was allowed to come!

As we then see from verse 7:2, Amos was led of God to intercede on behalf of the people under judgment here, as he saw the total devastation that the swarm of locust would cause, with our then seeing from verse 7:3 that God listened to Amos and did not allow this vision to become reality, again keeping in mind that the vision was allowed of God as a warning to the Northern kingdom of Israel!

We are to see that when Amos was led to say to God at verse 7:2, "How can Jacob stand, for he is small?," he was referring to the Northern kingdom of Israel in the word "Jacob," and to the fact that it was helpless and truly inconsequential when compared with God, with Whom it here had to do!

Amos 7:4-6, God gives Amos a second vision of calamity being planned, as a warning!

We then see from verses 7:4-6 that God gives Amos a second vision of calamity being planned, as a warning to the Northern kingdom of Israel, noting now what we there read, *"[4] Thus the Lord God showed me, and behold, the Lord God was calling to contend with them by fire, and it consumed the great deep and began to consume the farm land. [5] Then I said, "Lord God, please stop! How can Jacob stand, for he is small?" [6] The Lord changed His mind about this. "This too shall not be," said the Lord God."*

The second vision that God now gives Amos at verse 7:4 was of a fire about to burn the farm land, which would have affected their ability to sustain themselves, after the fire had caused all the water deposits to dry up, which would have been normally used in fighting the fire. And again, we see Amos here intercede on behalf of the people, with God again relenting by not causing the vision to become a reality!

Amos 7:7-9, God gives Amos a third vision, of what He has planned, which will now become a reality!

As we then see from Amos 7:7-9, God now not only gives Amos a third vision of what He has planned, but this time the vision will become a reality, noting now what we there read, *"[7] Thus He showed me, and behold, the Lord was standing by a vertical wall with a plumb line in His hand. [8] The Lord said to me, "What do you see, Amos?" And I said, "A plumb line." Then the Lord said, "Behold I am about to put a plumb line in the midst of My people Israel. I will spare them no longer. [9] The high places of Isaac will be desolated and the sanctuaries of Israel laid waste. Then I will rise up against the house of Jeroboam with the sword."*

In God's third vision to Amos here at verses 7:7,8, it is God Himself in a Theophany (appearing in His Son in a temporary physical body), Who appeared standing by a wall with a plumb line in His Hand. We are to be aware here that a plumb line was a cord with a lead weight at one end that was used in the erection of a building, in that it was used to ensure that the first wall and then all the walls were erected in accordance to specifications.

And so, in God placing a plumb line among those of the Northern kingdom of Israel was figurative here and meant that God had judged them in accordance with His word and had found them to have gone far from Him. Therefore, just as one tears down a wall that is not in accordance to specifications, so too will God 'tear down,' in that He will bring a total devastation on the Northern kingdom of Israel, and then they will go into exile, as we see Him say again here at verses 7:9,11. The mention of Jeroboam here at verse 7:9 spoke of the king of the Northern kingdom of Israel reigning at the time of Amos!

Amos 7:10-17, Amaziah, a priest at Bethel, tries to prevent Amos prophesying to the Northern kingdom of Israel, which results in his incurring God's judgment on him and his family!

What is then not surprising to see from Amos 7:10-17 is that opposition arises to Amos' prophesying from a priest at Bethel, which results in God's judgment falling on him and his family, as we there now read, "*[10] Then Amaziah, the priest of Bethel, sent word to Jeroboam king of Israel, saying, "Amos has conspired against you in the midst of the house of Israel; the land is unable to endure all his words. [11] For thus Amos says, 'Jeroboam will die by the sword and Israel will certainly go from its land into exile.' " [12] Then Amaziah said to Amos, "Go, you seer, flee away to the land of Judah and there eat bread and there do your prophesying! [13] But no longer prophesy at Bethel, for it is a sanctuary of the king and a royal residence." [14] Then Amos replied to Amaziah, "I am not a prophet, nor am I the son of a prophet; for I am a herdsman and a grower of sycamore figs. [15] But the Lord took me from following the flock and the Lord said to me, 'Go prophesy to My people Israel.' [16] Now hear the word of the Lord: you are saying, 'You shall not prophesy against Israel nor shall you speak against the house of Isaac.' [17] Therefore, thus says the Lord, 'Your wife will become a harlot in the city, your sons and your daughters will fall by the sword, your land will be parceled up by a measuring line and you yourself will die upon unclean soil. Moreover, Israel will certainly go from its land into exile.' ""*

Then as we see from verses 7:10,11, a priest at Bethel, by the name of Amaziah, sent word to Jeroboam, king of Israel, to let him know that Amos was prophesying things that were detrimental to his rule over the Northern kingdom, to the effect that Jeroboam himself would soon die by the sword and the kingdom over which he ruled would soon go into exile, not exactly the type of prophesy that would excite a king's ears!

And so, it is not surprising to see Amaziah at verse 7:12,13 confront Amos as He was prophesying this third vision there at Bethel, likely opposing Amos here as authorized by Jeroboam, letting him know that he was not welcome there, and should return to the land of Judah, since Bethel was a place of worship and also a place where the king had a residence.

We then note from verse 7:14,15 that Amos tells Amaziah that he should not call him a prophet, another term for a seer (noting 1 Samuel 9:9; 2 Samuel 24:11), as what Amaziah had referred to him at verse 7:12, but simply as a herdsman and a farmer, whom God had taken from his day to day work duties and had sent him out to prophesy to the Northern kingdom of Israel. In other words, Amos was here giving a defense of his ministry, as being of God, and not from himself!

And now, as a result of Amaziah arising and opposing one whom God Himself had sent to them, he would be judged by God for this, which is now the message from God that Amos relates to him at verses 7:16,17, where we see four things that will now happen to him and his family! One, his wife will become a harlot, which was a double blow to one who was supposedly a priest. Secondly, his sons and daughters were sure to die by the sword, once God did bring Assyria against the Northern kingdom of Israel. Thirdly, at that time of God's judgment, his own land will be parceled out to others, and fourthly, he himself will die on foreign soil, for as Amos was led of God to conclude here, the Northern kingdom of Israel had now definitely been consigned to exile!

CHAPTER EIGHT

Amos 8:1-14

Amos 8:1-3, God gives Amos a fourth vision of calamity that was now sure to come on the Northern kingdom of Israel!

As God continues His prophetic word through Amos, we note from Amos 8:1-3 that He now gives Amos a fourth vision of calamity that was now sure to come on the Northern kingdom of Israel, noting what we now there read, *"[1] Thus the Lord God showed me, and behold, there was a basket of summer fruit. [2] He said, "What do you see, Amos?" And I said, "A basket of summer fruit." Then the Lord said to me, "The end has come for My people Israel. I will spare them no longer. [3] The songs of the palace will turn to wailing in that day," declares the Lord God. "Many will be the corpses; in every place they will cast them forth in silence.""*

God has declared Himself in His word as both patient and merciful (noting 2 Peter 3:9; Luke 6:36), but that patience and mercy only extends so far! God has to eventually judge sin, or else He would not be true to His justice as a Lawmaker and Judge over His creation (James 4:12)! That is why we see God say to Amos here at verse 8:2, after giving him a vision of a basket of summer fruit at verse 8:1, "The end has come for My people Israel. I will spare them no longer." All the Northern kingdom of Israel had done since its beginning was sin against God, and now God was going to act!

A basket of summer fruit here was an indication that the yearly harvest was now complete. And similarly, in a spiritual sense, the Northern kingdom of Israel was at the end of their lack of fruitfulness in occupying the land, and now their end would come, in that they would be exiled (gathered) away from the land! And when that happens, as we see at verse 8:3, there will no longer be songs coming from the palace at Samaria, but rather now there will be corpses everywhere one looks!

What is important for us to grasp here is that God is not only the foundation stone for anything built in time (noting 1 Corinthians 3:11; Ephesians 2:20); but He is also its architect (noting Hebrews 11:10)! What this means then is that the nation of Israel had been raised of God for His purpose, which was twofold, namely to give His word to the nations of the earth through the believers of the nation of Israel, and to bring His Son to earth through a believing virgin of the nation of Israel. So as the nation of Israel started going astray from Himself, God allowed it to be split into two kingdoms, with the believers being in the Southern kingdom of Judah, while the unbelievers were in the Northern kingdom of Israel. And now God was simply in the process of getting rid of one part, which was irretrievably infected by sin, and send them into exile, so as not to further influence the Southern kingdom of Judah on that same downward spiritual spiral!

Amos 8:4-10, God prophesies through Amos that a day of tremendous upheaval was coming, with God here saying why!

As we then see from Amos 8:4-10, God prophesies a coming day of tremendous upheaval, with God here saying why, as we there now read, *"[4] Hear this, you who trample the needy, to do away with the humble of the land, [5] saying, "When will the new moon be over, so that we may sell grain, and the sabbath, that we may open the wheat market, to make the bushel smaller and the shekel bigger, and to cheat with dishonest scales, [6] so as to buy the helpless for money and the needy for a pair of sandals, and that we may sell the refuse of the wheat?" [7] The Lord has sworn by the pride of Jacob, "Indeed, I will never forget any of their deeds. [8] Because of this will not the land quake and everyone who dwells in it mourn? Indeed, all of it will rise up like the Nile, and it will be tossed about and subside like the Nile of Egypt. [9] It will come about in that day," declares the Lord God, that I will make the sun go down at noon and make the earth dark in broad daylight. [10] Then I will turn your festivals into mourning and all your songs into lamentation; and I will bring sackcloth on everyone's loins and baldness on every head. And I will make it like a time of mourning for an only son, and the end of it will be like a bitter day."*

What would be helpful before we get into the Biblical text here is to be reminded of the fact that when Adam and Eve sinned against God for the first time, as we see at Genesis 3:1-6, the devil, who was a created angelic being, had already fallen into sin and had led a third of the angels into rebellion against God, before then being instrumental in leading Adam and Eve into sin!

What is also important to remember is that God had already given the rule of this earth and its non-human creation to Adam and Eve, as we see at Genesis 1:26! And so, when Adam and Eve sinned against God, they were at the same time siding with the devil, which further meant that the rule of this earth and its non-human creation now fell into the devil's hands, as we see at Luke 4:6 and 1 John 5:19!

What this means then relating to our present subject is that the devil has kept the unbelievers of this world in bondage to three major sins, which are pride, greed, and lust, as we see for instance at 1 John 2:15-17; while God always seeks to have those who are believers to not only be free of these major sins, but also of all sins, since one is now a child of God in salvation!

And God has also always wanted to have those who are believers to look after the helpless, and the poor and needy, and to take up their cause in this ungodly world, where God knew the poor, the needy, and the women and children in particular would be oppressed by the unbelievers of this world, who are under the control of the evil one!

And so, coming back now to God's prophetic word through Amos, we see from verses 8:4-6 that God points out these exact evil deeds taking place among those of the Northern kingdom of Israel, which deeds did prove that they were unbelievers! And for such deeds as not being willing to help the poor and needy, and the helpless, and instead being greedy through their dishonest business practices, the judgment of God was about to fall on them!

Those of the Northern kingdom of Israel had forgotten what God had said at Deuteronomy 15:7-11 regarding the poor and needy! So instead of caring for the poor and helpless, they looked ahead for when their spiritual obligations toward God would be over, which for them as unbelievers were but rituals with no inward spiritual reality, while they sought to serve their real god, which was the devil, through money! All their actions only added to their sins and only brought the wrath of God against them closer to reality!

As God then goes on to point out at verses 8:7-10, the time of God's judgment that was coming upon them was going to be a time of tremendous upheaval for those of the Northern kingdom of Israel, which God likens here to the rising and falling of the waters of the Nile in Egypt, which would bring great mourning among the people, as they see physical phenomena that they have never seen before take place, such as the sun going down at noon and the earth becoming dark while it is still day. Their feast days would not then be for jubilation, but rather now will be a time of lamentation as for an only son. In short, the time of God's judgment that was coming would be a bitter time for all those of the Northern kingdom of Israel who have persisted in their unbelief and evil practices, while refusing to turn to God!

Amos 8:11-14, God here prophesies a coming day when there will be a famine in the land, not of food or water, but rather for the hearing of God's word!

What is then instructive to see from Amos 8:11-14 is that God now prophesies a famine in the land, not of food or water, but rather for the hearing of God's word, noting now what we there read, *"[11] Behold, days are coming," declares the Lord God, "when I will send a famine on the land, not a famine for bread or a thirst for water, but rather for hearing the words of the Lord. [12] People will stagger from sea to sea and from the north even to the east; they will go to and fro to seek the word of the Lord, but they will not find it. [13] In that day the beautiful virgins and the young men will faint from thirst. [14] As for those who swear by the guilt of Samaria, who say, 'As your god lives, O Dan,' and, 'As the way of Beersheba lives,' they will fall and not rise again.""*

What is important to see from what God says at verses 8:11,12, in terms of there being a famine that was coming upon the Northern kingdom of Israel for the hearing God's word, is that once God's judgment does fall on them, as when Assyria does come to devastate the land and take them all captive into exile, then the door to God will be shut, and God will no longer be listening to them at that time, no matter how many times they cry out to him, or no matter how far they travel in the land to try to find Him! The reality they were to grasp is that God was reaching out to them every time He was sending a prophet to them, such as Amos. That was the time to turn to God and live in accordance with His word! It would be too late to do so once His judgment had come upon them!

As we then see from verse 8:13,14, when God's judgment does fall, even those who are at their peak physically, such as the young men and virgins, will faint, not able to bear under what will be occurring. However, God's judgment at that time will be especially severe for those of the land who still look to their idols for protection and guidance. These will fall with their idols, never to rise or be seen again! Those of the Northern kingdom of Israel needed to heed now the truth which God relates at Hebrews 10:31, "It is a fearful thing to fall into the hands of the living God."

CHAPTER NINE

Amos 9:1-15

Amos 9:1-4, God here points out that when His judgment does come, those of the Northern kingdom of Israel will seek to escape His time of judgment, but none will escape it!

As God continues His prophetic word through Amos, He is now very emphatic at Amos 9:1-4 that when His judgment does come against the Northern kingdom of Israel, there will be none who will be able to escape it, no matter how hard they try, noting now what we there read, *"[1] I saw the Lord standing beside the altar, and He said, "Smite the capitals so that the thresholds will shake, and break them on the heads of them all! Then I will slay the rest of them with the sword; they will not have a fugitive who will flee, or a refugee who will escape. [2] Though they dig into Sheol, from there will My hand take them; and though they ascend to heaven, from there will I bring them down. [3] Though they hide on the summit of Carmel, I will search them out and take them from there; and though they conceal themselves from My sight on the floor of the sea, from there I will command the serpent and it will bite them. [4] And though they go into captivity before their enemies, from there I will command the sword that it slay them, and I will set My eyes against them for evil and not for good.""*

When Amos was led to say at verse 9:1 here, "I saw the Lord...," we are to see this as an appearance of God's Son in a Christophany, that is, a temporary preIncarnate appearance of Christ in the Old Testament. It is always good to remember that God The Father is always invisible, with His Son being the visible expression of the invisible God throughout time and eternity, noting Colossians 1:15!

And when we read that The Lord was "standing beside the altar," this would be in reference to the altar at Bethel, where God had Amos do his prophesying (noting verses 7:10-13), keeping in mind here that Bethel was at that time a place of idol worship.

Then when God says at verse 9:1, "Smite the capitals so that the thresholds will shake," we are to see that the word "capitals" referred to an ornamental piece on top of a pillar or column, while the word "thresholds" referred to the doorposts. And so, God was here calling for the smashing of the capitals so hard that the doorposts will shake and even break, as a way of indicating here the destruction of these altars at Bethel, and elsewhere in the Northern kingdom of Israel, once God's time of judgment had come upon them!

God further points out here at verse 9:1 that when His time of judgment comes, all those involved in that idol worship will lose their lives at His Hand! And when God speaks of the "fugitive" here, he is speaking of one who thinks he has escaped and is in hiding; while a "refugee" here would be those who think they will have escaped, because now taking refuge in a foreign land. God here says here that even these will NOT escape His judgment when that time of judgment does come!

And in order to amplify the truth that God has just stated, we see Him give examples at verses 9:2-4, to make His point that it does not matter where one goes to in all of God's creation, God can reach even there, so that no one is ever away from His Hand of judgment, no matter if one is in the lowest part of the earth, which is Sheol, or the highest part of His creation, which is Heaven, nevertheless, they would not be away from His reach; even if try to hide themselves on Mount Carmel, or on the floor of the sea, even there they would not be beyond His reach; and even when the enemy that was coming takes them captive, He will still be able to have them killed by the sword! In short, the time to make things right with God was now, and not wait until His judgment falls!

Amos 9:5,6, God here again declares Who it is that these unbelievers were dealing with!

As God has done on a number of occasions already as part of His prophetic word through Amos (noting verse 4:13; 5:8,9), He here again at Amos 9:5,6 discloses to those Who were about to experience His Hand of judgment just Who it was they were dealing with, as we there now read, *"[5] The Lord God of hosts, The One who touches the land so that it melts, and all those who dwell in it mourn, and all of it rises up like the Nile and subsides like the Nile of Egypt; 6] The One who builds His upper chambers in the heavens and has founded His vaulted dome over the earth, He who calls for the waters of the sea and pours them out on the face of the earth, The Lord is His name."*

Here we again see God disclose just Who it is that these unbelievers had to deal with, as One Who could melt any part of this earth with His touch; as One Who could bring his human creation to mourning at any time; as One Who could make any part of this earth rise and fall like the Nile river in Egypt; as One Who establishes His dwelling place anywhere He desires in the heavens, while having its supports anchored on this earth; and as One Who had control over the water cycle, where the moisture from bodies of waters is gathered into clouds and brings rain on the earth, wherever He determines it to go. This is The One and only God Who can do this and with Whom they had to do!

Before going on, we should mention that the term "upper chambers" at verse 9:6 is one word in the Hebrew, that being "Maalah," and the term "vaulted dome" is also one word in the Hebrew original, that being "Aguddah." These two terms have proved to be enigmatic for Bible translators from the Hebrew into English, with a variety of interpretation with no real consensus. God's point here appears to be to want to convey the fact that He controls and has access to both the spiritual and physical worlds!

Amos 9:7-10, God here reminds the Northern kingdom of Israel that they are part of the nation of Israel, to whom God gave birth, and even though God is about to cause most to die by the sword, yet He promises not to make a complete end of them!

Even though God has declared Himself to be a merciful and gracious God (noting Psalm 86:15), there is a limit! And now at Amos 9:7-10, even though He discloses that He is about to severely deal with the Northern kingdom of Israel, He does promise not to bring about a complete end of them, as He reminds them that they are part of the nation of Israel, to whom He gave birth, as we there now read, *"[7] Are you not as the sons of Ethiopia to Me, O sons of Israel?" declares the Lord. "Have I not brought up Israel from the land of Egypt, and the Philistines from Caphtor and the Arameans from Kir? [8] Behold, the eyes of the Lord God are on the sinful kingdom, and I will destroy it from the face of the earth; nevertheless, I will not totally destroy the house of Jacob," declares the Lord. [9] For behold, I am commanding, and I will shake the house of Israel among all nations as grain is shaken in a sieve, but not a kernel will fall to the ground. [10] All the sinners of My people will die by the sword, those who say, 'The calamity will not overtake or confront us.'"*

As we see from verse 9:7 here, God reminds the Northern kingdom of Israel that He not only raised the nation of Israel for Himself, but rendered them as numerous as "the sons of Ethiopia" (noting 2 Chronicles 14:9); also reminding them here that He is The One Who brought the sons of Israel out of Egypt as a nation (noting Exodus 12:37,40,41), just as He has also done in bringing the Philistines from Caphtor (believed to be Crete), and the Arameans from Kir (a place on the Tigris river in Mesopotamia), to their present locations!

At verse 9:8, God promises that He will severely deal with the Northern kingdom of Israel, but will not make a complete end of them, in that they will continue to exist as a people. The word "destroy" here does mean to exterminate, generally, but in the case of the Northern kingdom of Israel here He simply indicates that it is "the sinful kingdom" that will be exterminated, and not the people themselves making up the Northern kingdom of Israel! In a coming day, there will no longer be a Northern kingdom of Israel!

God repeats again what He is about to do by way of illustration at verse 9:9, by pointing out that just as grain (wheat or barley) is shaken in a sieve to separate the chaff from the kernel, yet in the case of those of the Northern kingdom of Israel, none will escape God's judgment, as when a kernel might fall to the ground in the case of His illustration, for as God further points out at verse 9:10, when His time of judgment comes at the hands of Assyria, the unbelievers of the Northern kingdom of Israel will die by the sword, especially those who in their arrogance denied that God's judgment was coming upon them!

Amos 9:11-15, God here now prophesies that there is a day coming in the future when He will restore the nation of Israel to her land and bless them more than they have ever been blessed before in their past history!

As we then see from Amos 9:11-15, God here now prophesies that there is a day coming in the future when He will restore the nation of Israel to her land and bless them more than they have ever been blessed in their past history, noting now what we there read, *"[11] In that day I will raise up the fallen booth of David, and wall up its breaches; I will also raise up its ruins and rebuild it as in the days of old; [12] that they may possess the remnant of Edom and all the nations who are called by My name," declares the Lord who does this. [13] "Behold, days are coming," declares the Lord, when the plowman will overtake the reaper and the treader of grapes him who sows seed; when the mountains will drip sweet wine and all the hills will be dissolved. [14] Also I will restore the captivity of My people Israel, and they will rebuild the ruined cities and live in them; they will also plant vineyards and drink their wine, and make gardens and eat their fruit. [15] I will also plant them on their land, and they will not again be rooted out from their land which I have given them," says the Lord your God."*

What is very important to grasp here is that when God says at verse 9:11, "In that day...," and then God goes to specify what He will do, as we see from verses 9:11-15, God is here speaking of the time of the fourth age of time, which will be after His Son, The Lord Jesus Christ, has returned to earth again, at the second stage of His second coming from Heaven (noting Revelation 19:11-16), in order to rule as King in the Kingdom of Heaven over the nations of the earth for a duration of a 1000 years (Isaiah 9:7; Daniel 7:14; Luke 1:31-33; Revelation 20:4,6)!

It is during the fourth age of time that God "will raise the fallen booth of David," in reference to the fact that the house of David will be restored to its place of prominence in the land of Israel, after having suffered captivity, when the Southern kingdom of Judah was exiled to Babylon in 586 BC, after all the cities of Judah had been destroyed, including the city of Jerusalem and God's temple there (noting Isaiah 16:9)! God will also at that time "wall up its breaches," in that no enemies will ever come and conquer them again, and He will rebuild the land again to more than match its former glory!

It is during the fourth age of time that the nation of Israel – which will at that time have had its two kingdoms of South and North reunited again under king David, who will have been resurrected from the dead to reign again over a united nation of Israel (noting Jeremiah 30:3-11; Ezekiel 37:15-28; Hosea 3:4,5) – will "possess" what is left of Edom at that time and of all the nations, which will all at that time be "called by My name," which is what God declares here at verse 9:12. It is very important to grasp here that the word "possess" refers to the fact that all nations on earth will belong to God's Kingdom of Heaven, which means that they will be under God's control and authority during the fourth age of time, noting Obadiah 1:15-21 here!

Then what God says at verses 9:14,15 is also what will happen during the fourth age of time, in that the descendants of those exiled from the Northern kingdom of Israel, along with the descendants of those exiled from the Southern kingdom of Judah, including those exiled during the reign of terror under the antichrist and his forces during the second half of the seven year tribulation period yet to come (noting Zechariah 14:2,5), these will all be brought back to the land of Israel by God's Son, The Lord Jesus Christ, once He returns to rule over the nations of the earth as King in the Kingdom of Heaven, never to be uprooted from the land that God had given them (noting Psalm 53:6; Isaiah 60:4; Jeremiah 30:3; Matthew 24:29-31).

During the 1000 year duration of the fourth age of time, when God will be ruling over all the nations of the earth through His Son from the holy city, Jerusalem, which will have come down from Heaven (noting Revelation 21:10), there will never again be war between nations (noting Isaiah 2:2-4), so that people throughout the earth, including those of the nation of Israel, will live as God intended mankind to live on earth when He brought the original creation into being!!

To God alone be all praise, honor, and glory, with thanksgiving, both now and forevermore! Amen, amen, and amen.

ADDENDUM A

The four ages of time

What is important to know when reading God's word, the Bible, is that God has divided time into four ages. And since God's word covers all of time, then all of God's word can be subdivided along the lines of these four ages. But before noting what these four ages are, we need to also be aware that in each of the four ages of time, God uses the believers of that age as His vessels. In other words, God is accomplishing His work on earth through the believers of each age of time.

And what is also important to keep in mind in regards to this is that although God starts each age with believers, before long the number of unbelievers in each age outnumbers the number of believers. In other words, one characteristic of each age of time is that there is a believing remnant among a mass of unbelievers, with these believers in each age being those whom God preserves for Himself and through whom God works to accomplish His purposes in each age through time.

And so, in the first age of time God worked through Adam and his believing descendants as His vessels to accomplish His will on earth, which age covers the first eleven chapters of Genesis. What this means is that they were the believers who willingly served Him out of love for Him. In other words, this was the believing line of descent, or the believing remnant, through which God worked out His will.

Then when we begin Genesis 12, we see God take one believer, Abraham, and out of that one man's descendants through the line of Isaac, and then through the line of Jacob, God makes a nation, which is Israel. And again, we need to see that only the believing line of descent within the nation of Israel was the remnant through which God worked to accomplish His will. What this means is that not all those who were of the nation of Israel were believers. In fact, the majority were unbelievers. Therefore, in the second age of time, which goes from Genesis 12 to the end of Malachi in the Old Testament, and includes the gospel accounts of Matthew, Mark, Luke, and John, plus Acts 1 and Revelation 6 to 19 in the New Testament, God works out His will in time through the believers of the nation of Israel, which is again a small number compared to the total number.

And here we need to pause for a moment and mention something else before going on to consider the third age of time, and this is the fact of representation. What this means is that in the first age of time, we have Adam and Eve as our first parents, who were but representative of all people on earth. In other words, God knew that what this one couple did, any other couple would have done the same thing, since God knows that once sin entered His perfect and sinless creation, we all would have the same sinful nature as human beings.

Then the same is true in regards to the nation of Israel in the second age of time, in that God knew that what this one nation did, any other nation on earth would likewise have done had it been chosen by God as a representative nation. So when God set out to make the one nation of Israel, He started out with just believers. But when the nation of Israel came into existence later, only a believing remnant within the nation were believers. Now since the nation of Israel was but representative of all the nations, then God knew that if He had chosen any other nation on earth, He would find that only a believing remnant would ever become believers to serve Him willingly out of love for Him out of a mass of unbelievers, who would now be in any of those nations. In other words, no other human being would have acted any differently than our first parents, and likewise, no other nation would have acted any differently than the nation of Israel did. This means that all human beings and all nations are likewise guilty before God!

What also needs to be mentioned here, as we now go on to look at the third age of time, is that the first two ages basically relate to the time period covered by the Old Testament, which means that the third and fourth ages of time must be covered by the New Testament portion of God's word, the Bible. And let us recall that in the first age, God worked through the believers of that age, beginning with Adam, while in the second age of time, God works through the believers of the nation of Israel, beginning with Abraham. So as we come to the third age of time, which goes from Acts 2 to the end of Revelation 5 in God's word, we have God working through all the believers of earth, whom God calls "the church."

What this means then is that in this third age of time, which we are presently still in, God is accomplishing His will through all the believers of earth, with God now not looking at any specific nation in particular. In other words, during the present third age of time, also known as 'the church age,' the nation of Israel, although being supernaturally preserved by God, is still just the same as any other nation on earth, having a believing remnant among a majority of unbelievers.

Then in the fourth age of time, which is basically covered by Revelation 20 to 22 in the New Testament, although mentioned often in prophecy in various portions of the Old Testament, we have God working through the believers of that age, but now with much greater variation. In other words, during the fourth age of time God works through the believers of every nation on earth still in their natural bodies, and also through the believers of the first three ages of time, who would have now experienced their part in the first resurrection relating to believers and who are now in their resurrected bodies! This is covered in much greater detail in my book, "An Introduction To The New World That Is Coming Upon The Earth," which focuses on this fourth age of time. If there are any readers who are not sure of what is meant by the first and second resurrection, and the fact of people serving God in their new resurrected bodies in the future, please see my book, "Have You Ever Wondered What Happens After Death?"

Before leaving this Addendum, it is also important to be aware that the Old Testament portion of God's word, the Bible, contains 39 books, which deal with the beginning of all things in God's plan of the ages, while the New Testament portion of God's word, the Bible, contains 27 books, which deal with the consummation of all things in God's eternal plan, which God is outworking through the four ages of time.

Also of great value is to know that the second age of time is not completed until AFTER the completion of the present third age of time. In other words, there are seven years remaining in the second age of time dealing with the nation of Israel, which is why this nation is being supernaturally preserved by God during this present third age, simply because God is not yet finished outworking His plan of the ages through the believers of that nation. These seven years remaining is a time of God's judgment against all unbelievers of earth and is approximately covered by Revelation 6:1 to Revelation 19:21 in God's word, although also mentioned often in prophecy in the Bible.

What also needs to be mentioned and is important to remember is that the reason God has a series of ages in time is in order to show us just how sinful the human race is and just how incapable it is of doing good, in terms of pleasing God on its own apart from God. What is meant here is that God's revelation of Himself increases as time progresses, so that those living in the fourth age of time, as compared to the first age of time, will have a far greater knowledge of God.

In other words, as each age progresses, God makes it easier and easier for human beings on earth to come to know Him and to serve Him out of love for Him. For example, in the first two ages, God's precious Son had not yet come to earth, so that He was foreshadowed only through types, such as the animal sacrifices and offerings, and in prophecy. Human beings at that time also only had the Old Testament as light to guide them.

But by the time we reach the fourth age of time, God's precious Son will not only have come from Heaven to earth bodily, but will actually be in the city just above the earth that God will have brought down from Heaven to start the fourth age (noting Revelation 20:10), reigning over the nations as King from there!

Please note what God says at Isaiah 11:9 in part, as just one example of what it will be like in the fourth age, which is something that could not be said in any prior age, "...For the earth will be full of the knowledge of the Lord as the waters cover the sea." What this means then is that when God's final judgment of time comes, relating to all the unbelievers of time (noting Revelations 20:11-15), then none of these unbelievers of time will be able to stand before God and give any excuse for their sin of unbelief, in having personally and freely rejected God's offer of salvation found in His own precious Son, The Lord Jesus Christ. And so, each succeeding age adds to mankind's culpability before a Holy and altogether Righteous God, so that in the end "every mouth may be closed and all the world may become accountable to God" (noting Romans 3:19 in part).

ADDENDUM B

The two comings from Heaven to earth of God's precious Son, our Lord Jesus Christ

Another very important truth to know here is that God's word, the Bible, mentions two comings of God's precious Son, The Lord Jesus Christ, from Heaven to earth. His first coming from Heaven to earth was for the purpose of taking on a body like ours, only in the innocence of Adam and as born of a virgin, so as not to incur our sinful nature; and then after living thirty-three and half years on earth carrying out only the will of God His Father in absolute sinlessness out of love for Him, was given over into the hands of unbelievers to be put to death on a cross, before being buried, then resurrected from the dead the third day. And of course, His death was not due to anything God's precious Son, The Lord Jesus Christ, had ever done wrong, but rather was to pay the penalty due the sins of the whole human race, which was death, in order that God might have a basis by which to forgive the sins and grant eternal life to those who come to believe in Him.

Then the second coming of God's precious Son is to be seen as being in two stages. The first stage of His second coming is at the end of this present third age of time, and is for the purpose of bringing to Heaven all believers of earth before God's judgment falls on the unbelievers of the earth, thereby bringing the present third age to a close. God has this first stage in view especially at 1 Thessalonians 4:14-17, although also mentioned in many portions of the New Testament.

Then the second stage of the second coming of God's precious Son, The Lord Jesus Christ, occurs at the end of the seven years of God's judgment, which will end the second age of time. God's precious Son would now be coming for one key battle against God's foes, as led by the devil, before establishing His reign on earth as King during the fourth age of time. This is again disclosed by God in many portions of God's word in the New Testament, but especially in passages such as Matthew 24 and Revelation 19:11-21.

ADDENDUM C

An exposition of how and for what purpose God raised up the nation of Israel in time!

What we are to now see in this Addendum is that STARTING AT GENESIS 12 AND GOING TO THE END OF ACTS 1, we have the start of THE SECOND AGE OF TIME, in which God does a new thing on the earth, in terms of raising up the nation of Israel for the purpose of now bringing His Son to the earth, as He had promised to do at Genesis 3:15! As the first age of time ended, God had desired to have believing nations on the earth, consisting of believers who would spread the knowledge of God and of His plan of salvation to others! Instead, what resulted on the earth was nations consisting of unbelievers in rebellion against God, as we see at Genesis 11, under the rulership of Satan, the devil, God's archenemy from the moment he sinned against God and started spreading a man-made, devil-inspired, false religious system on earth!

The raising up of the nation of Israel by God out of Abraham and his descendants

And so, instead of seeking to rule over His creation through Adam and his believing descendants, as God did during the first age of time, God now chooses one believer, ABRAHAM, and through him, HE RAISES UP THE NATION OF ISRAEL, WITH GOD THEN RULING OVER HIS CREATION FOR THE DURATION OF THE SECOND AGE OF TIME THROUGH THE BELIEVERS OF THE NATION OF ISRAEL. So just as Adam was REPRESENTATIVE of all human beings in the first age of time, now the nation of Israel that God now raises up through Abraham will also be REPRESENTATIVE of all the nations of the earth during the second age of time!

And so, just as God knew that what Adam and Eve did, any other couple would have also done in its place; so too now in the second age of time, God knows that whatever the nation of Israel does, any other nation would likewise have done, if that nation had been chosen instead of Israel as a representative nation. In other words, God knows that the soul of mankind has been totally corrupted by the sinful human nature that all human beings have all over the earth, since all humans are descended from Adam and Eve, the first parents of the whole of the human race, who incurred that sinful nature, which has been passed on from male to female at conception ever since.

And so, at Genesis 12:2, we see God tell Abram (whose name God later changed from “Abram” to “Abraham” at Genesis 17:5) what we now read, “And I WILL MAKE YOU A GREAT NATION, and I will bless you, and make your name great; and so you shall be a blessing…” We are then to see that God goes about making a great nation out of Abraham by first giving him a son, Isaac; as we see from Genesis 21:1-3, who was born to Abraham’s wife Sarah, while they were both quite advanced in age, “[1] Then the Lord took note of Sarah as He had said, and the Lord did for Sarah as He had promised. [2] So Sarah conceived and bore a son to Abraham in his old age, at the appointed time of which God had spoken to him. [3] Abraham called the name of his son who was born to him, whom Sarah bore to him, ISAAC.”

Then God continued His plan of making a nation out of Abraham by giving Isaac two sons through his wife Rebekah, one named Jacob and the other Esau, as we see from Genesis 25:20-26, “[20] and Isaac was forty years old when he took Rebekah, the daughter of Bethuel the Aramean of Paddan-aram, the sister of Laban the Aramean, to be his wife. [21] Isaac prayed to the Lord on behalf of his wife, because she was barren; and the Lord answered him and Rebekah his wife conceived. [22] But the children struggled together within her; and she said, "If it is so, why then am I this way?" So she went to inquire of the Lord. [23] The Lord said to her, "TWO NATIONS are in your womb; and two peoples will be separated from your body; and one people shall be stronger than the other; and the older shall serve the younger." [24] When her days to be delivered were fulfilled, behold, there were TWINS in her womb. [25] Now the first came forth red, all over like a hairy garment; and they named him ESAU. [26] Afterward his brother came forth with his hand holding on to Esau's heel, so his name was called JACOB; and Isaac was sixty years old when she gave birth to them."

But God was not yet finished making that one nation out of Abraham and his descendants, for then we see that God proceeded to give Jacob twelve sons, with God then changing Jacob's name to "ISRAEL," as we see at Genesis 32:28, "He said, "YOUR NAME SHALL NO LONGER BE JACOB, BUT ISRAEL; for you have striven with God and with men and have prevailed.""

However, a name change and twelve sons does not a nation make, but then God was not yet finished, for we see Him tell Jacob HOW He was to make that nation, when God says to Jacob at Genesis 46:2,3, whose name was now Israel, "[2] God spoke to Israel in visions of the night and said, "Jacob, Jacob." And he said, "Here I am." [3] He said, "I am God, the God of your father; DO NOT BE AFRAID TO GO DOWN TO EGYPT, FOR I WILL MAKE YOU A GREAT NATION THERE." And so we see that it was while Jacob, now called "Israel," was in Egypt with his family that God made "a great nation" out of Abraham and his descendants!

And in order to see HOW God now finalized the making of the nation of Israel through Abraham and his descendants, we are to note that God had worked in such a way that Joseph, one of Jacob's sons, was brought to Egypt and was now the second in command under Pharaoh, the king of Egypt. With Joseph being in charge of dispensing food supplies, there was a famine in the land where Jacob and his sons were, which was of course engineered by God in order to get Jacob and his sons to move to Egypt.

So Jacob, as Israel, obeys God, since he is a believer, and moves down to Egypt with his family after finding out that Joseph was still alive and was in Egypt. And so, Jacob, as now Israel, ends up living in Egypt, where his twelve sons and their descendants multiply greatly under God's direct intervention and protection for the next 430 years, with their then coming out of Egypt at the end of that time under MOSES, another believer chosen of God to now lead Israel and his descendants to the land promised them by God.

So let us note here what God tells us at Exodus 12:37,40,41 relating to what has just been said above about what occurred at the end of the 430 years in Egypt, "[37] Now THE SONS OF ISRAEL journeyed from Rameses to Succoth, about six hundred thousand men on foot, aside from children... [40] Now the time that THE SONS OF ISRAEL lived in Egypt was four hundred and thirty years. [41] And at the end of four hundred and thirty years, to the very day, all the hosts of the Lord went out from the land of Egypt."

Now we are to see that those six hundred thousand men, not counting the women and children, who were all the descendants of Israel, were now coming out of Egypt as THE NATION OF ISRAEL, on their way to the land of Canaan, which God had promised to give them, and which, when possessed later under Joshua's leadership, would then BECOME THE LAND OF ISRAEL.

The giving of God's written word to the nations of the world through the nation of Israel

What we are to now see is that one primary reason for God RAISING UP THE NATION OF ISREAEL was for God to have a nation of believers on earth, and through that one nation to spread the knowledge of God, and especially the knowledge of how to have a personal relationship with God through faith in His Son, to all the other nations of the earth. And so, early in Israel's history as a nation, God gave them HIS WRITTEN WORD, starting with Moses. During the first age of time, man had been passing on the knowledge of God ORALLY; and now for the first time in history, we have God's word being transmitted IN WRITTEN FORM THROUGH THE BELIEVERS OF THE NATION OF ISRAEL!

God prepares the nation of Israel, and through them the nations of the earth, for the coming to earth of His Son, as God had promised at Genesis 3:15, by giving signs for them to recognize when His Son came, as born of a woman

Then the second primary reason for God raising up the nation of Israel was for the purpose of bringing His Son to earth, as He had promised to do at Genesis 3:15. However, what we are first to see and what should not be surprising, due to the fact that human beings do have a sinful nature inherited from our first father Adam, is that as the years progressed, the descendants of the believers that God used to first bring about the nation of Israel, namely Abraham, Isaac, Jacob and his twelve sons, started going astray from God, which led God to raise one PROPHET after another in order to bring the nation of Israel back to God, as is clear from what God tells us at Jeremiah 7:25,26, "[25] Since the day that your fathers came out of the land of Egypt until this day, I HAVE SENT YOU ALL MY SERVANTS THE PROPHETS, daily rising early and sending them. [26] YET YOU DID NOT LISTEN TO ME (that is, did not obey) or incline their ear, but stiffened their neck; they did more evil than their fathers."

And another reason for God raising the prophets that we see throughout the Old Testament, from Moses onward, was to instruct the nation of Israel, as representative of the nations of the earth, how to serve God by carrying out His will while on earth, and especially to prepare them all for the coming of His Son by giving them SIGNS, so that when God's Son came to earth, as promised by God at Genesis 3:15, then they would be able to recognize Him. And so, for instance, we see at Deuteronomy 18:15 that God promised the nation of Israel through Moses that He would one day send them a prophet, having now His Son in view, "The Lord your GOD WILL RAISE UP FOR YOU A PROPHET like me from among you, from your countrymen, you shall listen to him."

Then later, one important sign that God gave through the prophet Isaiah, regarding His coming Son, was that He would be BORN OF A VIRGIN. In other words, now in the second age of time, God was making known that the "woman" that God had promised to send His Son through, at Genesis 3:15 during the first age of time, would be a virgin, noting what God tells us at Isaiah 7:14, "Therefore the Lord Himself will give you a sign: Behold, a VIRGIN will be with child and bear A SON, and SHE WILL CALL HIS NAME IMMANUEL." That word "Immanuel" here is the Hebrew word "Immanue-el," meaning 'God is with us.'

Then through the prophet Micah, God made known that His Son would be born in Bethlehem, in the land of Israel, which meant that the virgin woman would herself be of the nation of Israel; with God also making known at the same time that His Son would have the rule over Israel, noting what we read at Micah 5:2, “But as for you, BETHLEHEM Ephrathah, too little to be among the clans of Judah, from you One will go forth for Me to be RULER IN ISRAEL. His goings forth are from long ago, from the days of eternity."

But then we note that not only would God’s Son be ruling over Israel one day, as prophesied above by Micah, but that He actually would be coming to them as King, when He came to earth at His first coming, noting what God foretold through the prophet at Zechariah 9:9, “Rejoice greatly, O daughter of Zion! Shout in triumph, O daughter of Jerusalem! Behold, YOUR KING IS COMING TO YOU; He is just and endowed with salvation, Humble, and mounted on a donkey, even on a colt, the foal of a donkey.”

What we are to also see here is that there were two sets of prophecies, as signs, that God gave about His coming Son during the second age of time that threw a curve ball to the believers of the nation of Israel, which caused them some perplexity, as we will now see. First then, we note from 1 Chronicles 17:10b-14 what God told David, who was king over the nation of Israel, “[10b] Moreover, I tell you that the Lord will build a house for you. [11] When your days are fulfilled that you must go to be with your fathers, that I WILL SET ONE OF YOUR DESCENDANTS after you, who will be of your sons; and I WILL ESTABLISH HIS KINGDOM. [12] He shall build for Me a house, and I WILL ESTABLISH HIS THRONE FOREVER. [13] I will be his father and he shall be My son; and I will not take My lovingkindness away from him, as I took it from him who was before you. [14] But I will settle him in My house and in My kingdom forever, and HIS THRONE SHALL BE ESTABLISHED FOREVER."

Then secondly, God made known to the nation of Israel, and through them to the nations of the earth, what we now read at Isaiah 53, followed by what we read at Psalm 22, which also related to God’s coming Son and caused them perplexity, noting here first Isaiah 53:2-9, “[2] For He grew up before Him like a tender shoot, and like a root out of parched ground; He has no stately form or majesty that we should look upon Him, nor appearance that we should be attracted to Him. [3] He was despised and forsaken of men, a man of sorrows and acquainted with grief; and like one from whom men hide their face He was despised, and we did not esteem Him. [4] Surely our griefs He Himself bore, and our sorrows He carried; yet we ourselves esteemed Him stricken, smitten of God, and afflicted. [5] But HE WAS PIERCED THROUGH FOR OUR TRANSGRESSIONS, HE WAS CRUSHED FOR OUR INIQUITIES; the chastening for our well-being fell upon Him, and by His scourging we are healed. [6] All of us like sheep have gone astray, each of us has turned to his own way; but THE LORD HAS CAUSED THE INIQUITY OF US ALL TO FALL ON HIM. [7] He was oppressed and He was afflicted, yet He did not open His mouth; like a lamb that is led to slaughter, and like a sheep that is silent before its shearers, so He did not open His mouth. [8] By oppression and judgment He was taken away; and as for His generation, who considered that HE WAS CUT OFF OUT OF THE LAND OF THE LIVING FOR THE TRANSGRESSION OF MY PEOPLE TO WHOM THE STROKE WAS DUE? [9] His GRAVE was assigned with wicked men, Yet He was with a rich man IN HIS DEATH, because He had done no violence, nor was there any deceit in His mouth."

We then note from Psalm 22:14-18 what God had also said regarding His coming Son, "[14] I am poured out like water, and all my bones are out of joint; My heart is like wax; it is melted within me. [15] My strength is dried up like a potsherd, and my tongue cleaves to my jaws; and You lay me in the dust of DEATH. [16] For dogs have surrounded me; a band of evildoers has encompassed me; THEY PIERCED MY HANDS AND MY FEET. [17] I can count all my bones. they look, they stare at me; [18] They divide my garments among them, and for my clothing they cast lots."

And so we see that on the one hand God was telling the nation of Israel that His coming Son would rule over the nation as their King, with His throne and kingdom being established forever; while on the other hand, God was telling the nation of Israel that when His Son came to earth, He would die in the place of the sinful human race, bearing their sins. And of course, this caused perplexity in the minds of all believers of the second age of time, up to the time of the actual coming to earth of God's precious Son took place, simply because they were not aware that there would be A FIRST AND A SECOND COMING OF GOD'S SON TO THE EARTH! God only revealed this fact AFTER His Son had actually come to earth as born of that woman, who was a virgin of the nation of Israel.

And so, about forty years before the end of the second age of time – with what was just said above being only a preparation for this – we see that while the nation of Israel was again in unbelief, God now brings His Son from Heaven to earth, as promised at Genesis 3:15 in the first age of time! And this God would now do through the nation of Israel, that we have just seen Him bring into existence through the one man Abraham! And so, as the New Testament opens, which we need to remember is still in the second age of time, we read in the very first verse at Matthew 1:1, which verse is intended by God to carry us across the bridge from the Old Testament to the New Testament, noting now what God there declares, "The record of the genealogy of Jesus the Messiah, the son of David, the son of Abraham:"

The name "Jesus" is the human name that God's eternally-existing Son was given by God His Father to go along with His Name of Messiah, which word means "Christ," which Name God's Son already had when He came to earth at His first coming. So let us note what God tells us at John 1:40-42 in part, with what is in brackets here being part of God's word, "[40] One of the two who heard John speak and followed Him, was Andrew, Simon Peter's brother. [41] He found first his own brother Simon and said to him, "We have found the Messiah" (which translated means Christ). [42] He brought him to Jesus…"

So let us note for our present purpose that Jesus Christ, God's Son now visibly and permanently in a human body, was now on earth as A DESCENDANT OF ABRAHAM, whom we have seen God make the nation of Israel through! What this means then is that God's Son was now in a human body on earth as Jesus Christ, born of a virgin woman of the nation of Israel! But the story of what God was attempting to do here does not end there, for we also need to note that at Matthew 1:1 God also said that Jesus was also A DESCENDANT OF DAVID, whom we have already introduced as being the king of Israel that God had raised for Himself and to whom God had prophesied at 1 Chronicles 17:10b-14 to establish a house, a kingdom, and a throne through one of his descendants, which turned out to be God's Son, The Lord Jesus Christ!

And so, when God's Son was born of a virgin of the nation of Israel into this world , as conceived in her womb by God The Father (noting Hebrews 10:5), so as not to incur the sinful nature that all humans have, we are to first see that He was in fact the descendant promised to David back at 1 Chronicles 17:11, that God said would one day come, in direct line as a descendant of David and so as the rightful heir as KING over the nation of Israel, at His first coming from Heaven to earth, as is clear from what God told Mary, at Luke 1:31-33, who was that virgin woman of the nation of Israel, that God The Father brought His Son to this earth by, "[1] And behold, you will conceive in your womb and bear a son, and you shall name Him JESUS. [32] He will be great and will be called the Son of the Most High; and THE LORD GOD WILL GIVE HIM THE THRONE OF HIS FATHER DAVID; [33] AND HE WILL REIGN OVER THE HOUSE OF JACOB FOREVER, AND IS KINGDOM WILL HAVE NO END," and then also noting from Matthew 2:1,2 what God made known AFTER His birth into this world at His first coming, "[1] Now after Jesus was born in Bethlehem of Judea in the days of Herod the king, magi from the east arrived in Jerusalem, saying, [2] WHERE IS HE WHO HAS BEEN BORN KING OF THE JEWS? For we saw His star in the east and have come to worship Him."

But the unfortunate reality is that when God's Son finally came from Heaven to earth, which as mentioned above was about forty years BEFORE THE SECOND AGE OF TIME WAS INTERRUPTED BY GOD TO BRING IN THE PRESENT THIRD AGE OF TIME, the nation of Israel consisted of a majority of unbelievers at that point, with only a very small believing remnant. This is important to know since what God was attempting to do was to set up a kingdom on earth through His Son, The Lord Jesus Christ, as King over that kingdom, which would have been the fulfillment of what God promised to David at 1 Chronicles 17. That is why when God's Son started His public ministry at the age of thirty (noting Luke 3:23), He immediately began to preach to the nation of Israel what we read at Matthew 4:17, “From that time Jesus began to preach and say, "REPENT, FOR THE KINGDOM OF HEAVEN IS AT HAND."

God’s Son, now in human flesh, had to say “repent,” which meant to turn from one’s sins to God, to receive the forgiveness of sins, for as we have just stated, the nation of Israel was in unbelief at this time. And He was letting them know that “the kingdom of Heaven is at hand,” because this is what His Father desired to set up on earth, which was God’s rule through His Son as King over the nations of the earth through the representative nation of Israel in His kingdom on earth. However, since the nation of Israel was in unbelief, this meant that they did reject God’s Son as their King AT HIS FIRST COMING, which also meant that they refused to believe that The Lord Jesus Christ was God’s Son, no matter how many miracles He did in their sight!

And so the end result was that God was not able to establish the kingdom of Heaven on earth through His Son as King AT HIS FIRST COMING from Heaven to earth near the end of the second age of time, due to the leadership of the nation of Israel, as representing the nation, being in unbelief, and so is why they turned Him over to the Romans (who ruled over the nation of Israel at this time) in order to be crucified, noting what they finally say to Pilate, the Roman governor, at John 19:14,15, “[14] Now it was the day of preparation for the Passover; it was about the sixth hour. And he (Pilate) said to the Jews, "Behold, your KING!" [15] So they cried out, "Away with Him, away with Him, crucify Him!" Pilate said to them, "Shall I crucify your KING?" The chief priests answered (as representing the nation of Israel in unbelief), "WE HAVE NO KING BUT CAESAR." “

And here again, we need to see that this did not mean that God had failed in not being able to establish His rule on earth through His Son as King over His kingdom at His first coming to earth. We must remember that God knows the end before the beginning of all things, so here again God knew what the nation of Israel in unbelief would do to His Son when He came at His first coming from Heaven to earth, in that they would crucify Him on a cross, that He would be buried, and then raised from the dead the third day, which God would use as a basis to bring the forgiveness of sins and eternal life to all those who would look back now to the cross and believe in His Son, The Lord Jesus Christ!

As we have seen from Isaiah 53 and Psalm 22, parts of which we have already quoted, God knew in advance what sinful mankind in unbelief would do to His Son when He came at His first coming to earth, which shows that God is even able to take the sinful acts of men and use it for His purpose! And here we can note what God tells us at Acts 2:22-24, "[22] Men of ISRAEL, listen to these words: JESUS the Nazarene, a man attested to you by God with miracles and wonders and signs which God performed through Him in your midst, just as you yourselves know — [23] this Man, DELIVERED OVER BY THE PREDETERMINED PLAN AND FOREKNOWLEDGE OF GOD, you nailed to a cross by the hands of godless men and put Him to death. [24] But God raised Him up again, putting an end to the agony of death, since it was impossible for Him to be held in its power."

The reality to be seen here is that God still accomplished good for mankind, even though mankind in unbelief rejected and crucified unto death His Son on a cross, when He came at His first coming from Heaven to earth. For we are to see that just as God was able to bring the knowledge of salvation to mankind by saving Adam and Eve in the first age of time, then leaving that knowledge on earth to be passed on to others, NOW THROUGH HIS SON ACTUALLY COMING TO EARTH AT HIS FIRST COMING IN THE SECOND AGE OF TIME, THAT SALVATION WAS FOREVER PROVIDED FOR THROUGH HIS SON'S DEATH AT THE CROSS, HIS BURIAL, AND HIS RESURRECTION FROM THE DEAD THE THIRD DAY!

So what we are to remember here is that those of the first two ages of time, which is principally during the time of the Old Testament, were saved, that is, came into a personal relationship with God through believing in The Son of God, Who was promised as coming in the future, with His death, burial, and resurrection from the dead being pictured in the Old Testament through the animal sacrifices and offerings in particular. However, now in the third and fourth ages of time, which is principally during the time of the New Testament, one is saved, that is, comes into a personal relationship with God through looking back and believing in God's Son, Who has now come in real life to provide that salvation, through His death at the cross as payment due the sins of the human race, His burial, and His resurrection from the dead the third day!

We must further grasp that God knows exactly what He is doing through each of the ages of time, even though to us this may appear as a failure at first glance. And so, what God attempted to do in bringing His Son to earth at His first coming during the second age of time was not a failure, for God accomplished a completed salvation and much good for mankind. For as God goes on to tell us at 1 John 3:8, relating to the first coming to earth of His Son, "the one who practices sin is of the devil; for the devil has sinned from the beginning. THE SON OF GOD APPEARED FOR THIS PURPOSE (at His first coming), TO DESTROY THE WORKS OF THE DEVIL."

The works the devil brought to the human race was sin and death, which God's Son now undoes AT HIS FIRST COMING from Heaven to earth, noting also what God tells us at Hebrews 2:14,15,17, "[14] Therefore, since the children share in flesh and blood, He Himself likewise also partook of the same, that through death He might render powerless him who had the power of death, that is, the devil, [15] and might free those who through fear of death were subject to slavery all their lives… [17] Therefore, He had to be made like His brethren in all things, so that He might become a merciful and faithful high priest in things pertaining to God, to make propitiation (that is, be the acceptable sacrifice offered to God His Father in payment) for the sins of the people."

And so we see that God dealt with the sins of the human race through the death of His Son, The Lord Jesus Christ, when He bore the sins of humankind in His own body on the cross (noting 1 Peter 2:24) and was buried in order to put away the sins of mankind from God's sight forever, as God makes clear at 1 John 3:5, "You know that He appeared in order to take away sins; and in Him there is no sin," and also at Hebrews 9:26 in part, "…now once at the consummation of the ages He has been manifested to put away sin by the sacrifice of Himself." And then God did away with death through God's Son when He raised Him from the dead the third day, with death finally being eliminated for mankind also when God raises all believers of the four ages of time through the first resurrection, and then with all unbelievers of time being raised from the dead all at once to face God at the final judgment of time, as we see at Revelation 20:11-15.

ADDENDUM D

The nature of man and the consequence of sin!

What will here be provided are basic truths on the nature of man as originally created by God, and what we all became as a result of the sin of Adam. And so, the first basic truth to be aware of is that the first man created by God, whom God called "Adam," the woman that God then created to be his wife, and who was named "Eve," were actual people, and are the original couple from which the whole human race comes from.

What is also important to remember is that Adam and Eve were not only actual people, but were also representative of the whole human race, meaning that any other man or woman in existence after them would have done the very same as they did, had they been in their place, and would not have acted any differently than they did. In other words, God created us all with a like nature, so that what one does under a certain set of circumstances, then all will likewise do under the same set of circumstances, due to the initial makeup of our human nature by God. And so we are to see that all mankind has the same composition and nature, in that each human being comes from the same man and woman God first created.

Therefore, the second basic truth we need to be aware of is what the constituent parts of man were as first created by God, noting here what we are told at Genesis 2:7, when God first created Adam, "Then the Lord God formed man of dust from the ground, and breathed into his nostrils the breath of life; and man became a living being."

What we are to see from this verse of the Bible is that the constituent parts of man consist of a body, "formed… of dust" by God, into which God "breathed into his nostrils the breath of life," which is the human spirit, so that man "became a living being," that is, a living soul. And these then are the three constituent parts of man that God speaks about in His word, as we see for instance at 1 Thessalonians 5:23, where we read, "Now may the God of peace Himself sanctify you entirely; and may your SPIRIT AND SOUL AND BODY be preserved complete, without blame at the coming of our Lord Jesus Christ."

What is then important to know is that God gave the human spirit for man to be able to commune with God, Who is revealed in the Bible as being a spirit Being, noting what we read at John 4:24, "God is spirit, and those who worship Him must worship in spirit and truth."

This is how Adam was communing with God before he sinned, through his spirit, or we could say 'spiritually.' At that point, there was as yet no sin in Adam to prevent his communing with God by his spirit, that is, spiritually. Although, all of that would change the moment Adam sinned against God.

We are then to see that the "soul" is the human part of man, being the component of our being which renders us a person, and which God gave man so as to be able to commune with other human beings. It is the soul of man that contains our will, our mind, our emotions, our heart, and our conscience. There is also a heart of the body, which is the organ which pumps our blood to keep us alive physically. In contrast to this, the heart of the soul is the inner part of the soul of man, while the human spirit is the inner part of the whole human being.

And what is important to remember about the spirit, soul, and body at this point is that the spirit and soul are immaterial and unseen, while the body, is the only part of us that is material and can be seen, being the shell that holds the spirit and soul of man. Once created by God in the first man, Adam, and then passed on through childbirth, the spirit and soul never die, but go on for eternity! Only the human body ages and dies!

God had created Adam, as representative of the whole human race, in His own image so that man might be able to commune with God spiritually, that is, through one's human spirit. However, there came a day when God tested Adam, when He said to him in the garden of Eden, which was here on earth, as we now read at Genesis 2:16,17, "[16] The Lord God commanded the man, saying, "From any tree of the garden you may eat freely; [17] but from the tree of the knowledge of good and evil you shall not eat, for in the day that you eat from it you will surely die."

Unfortunately, there also came a day when Adam lost the state of innocence, which is the moment Adam disobeyed God's command above and did partake of the forbidden tree, noting now what we read at Genesis 3:1-6, [1] Now the serpent was more crafty than any beast of the field which the Lord God had made. And he said to the woman, "Indeed, has God said, 'You shall not eat from any tree of the garden'?" [2] The woman said to the serpent, "From the fruit of the trees of the garden we may eat; [3] but from the fruit of the tree which is in the middle of the garden, God has said, 'You shall not eat from it or touch it, or you will die.' " [4] The serpent said to the woman, "You surely will not die! [5] "For God knows that in the day you eat from it your eyes will be opened, and you will be like God, knowing good and evil." [6] When the woman saw that the tree was good for food, and that it was a delight to the eyes, and that the tree was desirable to make one wise, she took from its fruit and ate; and she gave also to her husband with her, and he ate."

The moment that Adam ate of that forbidden tree in the garden of Eden, he became not only a sinner by practice, but also a sinner by nature, in that all which came from Adam from that moment onward would be sin in God's sight, that is, all thoughts, actions, and words.

And so that is why that God needed to send His eternal and sinless Son from Heaven to earth to take on a body like we have, but in the innocence of Adam, and then after thirty-three years of life here on earth of living only by the righteousness of God, as a Pattern for us, He died in our place at the cross, for the penalty for sin, as we saw at Genesis 2:17, is death.

When one comes to believe in God through faith in His Son, The Lord Jesus Christ – namely that He died for our sins, was buried, and was raised again the third day – then one receives from God the forgiveness of sins (which includes every single sin committed from the age of accountability onward) and eternal life with Him. That eternal life is to be seen as God's own righteous life, or righteousness, so that when a believer lives by God's righteousness, then all one thinks, does, and says is right in God's sight.

Therefore, how important that the child of God see that from the moment of salvation onward, one who is now a child of God through salvation is no longer to live by one's self life, which is drawing life from the soul, which is now sinful by nature, as we have seen above; but rather now the one who is a child of God is to live by God's righteousness alone. One cannot be pleasing to God unless one is living by God's righteousness!

Then the last truth which is important to be aware of here as believers is that the sin of Adam and Eve had a consequence for the whole human race. And at this point, we need to mention again the fact that Adam was not only a literal human being, but Adam was also a representative man, in that through him, and what happens to him here, God then uses this to teach the whole of the human race about certain concepts, such as sin and death. That is why God says at Romans 5:12, "Therefore, just as through one man (Adam) sin entered into the world, and death through (Adam's) sin, and so death spread to all men, because all sinned (that is, all personally do at the age of accountability)..."

This is a very important verse, for here we learn that through Adam, as our representative man, who not only became a sinner by practice, but also a sinner by nature, and since we are all descendants of this one man, then all human beings incur at birth Adam's sinful nature, so that shortly after reaching the age of accountability – which is the age at which a child first learns right from wrong, and chooses the wrong, thereby becoming personally accountable to God for one's sin against Him – so that when one also sins against God, one not only becomes a sinner by practice, but also a sinner by nature.

All human beings can identify with the truth just stated. I know that when I was a child my parents did not have to teach me how to sin, as that came naturally! In fact, my parents constantly had to show me the right way, for of my own, I kept going astray from what was right. That is because I had reached the age of accountability and now had a sinful nature that only ever wanted to sin. If you are a parent, you have probably painfully noticed already that this is also true in your own children. There is nothing unusual happening here, we are only experiencing the consequence of Adam's sin, a sin, we must ever remember, that any of us would have also committed had we been in Adam's place, since he was but representative of us all. Therefore, as a consequence of Adams's sin, the whole human race not only became sinners by practice and by nature!

“Jesus said to him, “I am the way, and the truth, and the life; no one comes to the Father but through Me.” “

John 14:6

ADDENDUM E

For those who may not as yet know God

Possibly you have been reading this book and have become aware of not knowing this God Who created us and gave us physical life into this world, and up to now has allowed you to live on earth. However, now you do have the desire to know God in a personal way. If this is the case, then this Addendum has been written specifically for you!

And what God wants you to have in coming to know Him is the peace and joy, which comes in knowing that all of your sins committed in your lifetime are forgiven and that you have eternal life with God. And so, your greatest need at the moment is to make peace with God so as to go to Heaven, which is God's home. And so, this Addendum will help to bring that about by pointing you to God so as to come to know Him through faith in His Son, The Lord Jesus Christ.

As we begin, we need to note a most important promise which God makes at Romans 6:23 to all those who do not yet know Him, "For the wages of sin is death, but the free gift of God is eternal life in Christ Jesus our Lord." The good news here is that God offers you eternal life with Him as a free gift, which is to be obtained in His Son, Jesus Christ. What God does not do in this verse from the Bible is tell us 'how' to obtain that eternal life with Him.

Another verse which we can look at where God does let us know 'how' one can obtain that eternal life with Him is noting what God tells us at John 3:16, "For God so loved the world, that He gave His only begotten Son, that whoever believes in Him shall not perish, but have eternal life." Now the added truth which God makes known here is that the eternal life, which He gives to a human being as a free gift, is for those who believe in His Son.

Then the question is: What is it that I am to believe about God's Son, Jesus Christ, which will lead God to give me eternal life with Him forever? And the beauty of God is that He never leaves us guessing, especially when it comes to having a personal relationship with Him, which He desires us to have. Therefore, we should not be surprised when God gives us the answer to our question in what He tells us at 1 Corinthians 15:1-4, "[1] Now I make known to you, brethren, the gospel (which is God's good news regarding His Son) which I preached to you, which also you received, in which also you stand, [2] by which also you are saved, if you hold fast the word which I preached to you, unless you believed in vain. [3] For I delivered to you as of first importance what I also received, that Christ died for our sins according to the Scriptures, [4] and that He was buried, and that He was raised on the third day according to the Scriptures..."

Therefore, "the gospel," which simply means 'good news,' which God wants you to hear and believe in order to "be saved," which simply refers to you coming to know God and have eternal life with Him, is that His Son has already died for you, has already been buried, and has already been raised from the dead again the third day after His death, in order that God would have a basis by which to forgive you of all your sins, which are all against Him, and to freely give you eternal life with Him, for simply believing this message in your heart.

One thing which often prevents a person from believing the gospel at this point is not seeing oneself as a sinner before a Holy God. When we look at ourselves by our own assessment, and especially when we compare ourselves with others around us, we often think of ourselves as being better than others, and so good enough to enter Heaven in our present condition. The problem with this is that it is the product of our own thinking and is not God's assessment of our situation!

God's assessment of our situation is as He tells us at Romans 3:10-12,23 in part, "[10] as it is written, "There is none righteous, not even one... [11] there is none who seeks for God [12] all have turned aside... there is none who does good, there is not even one... [23] for all have sinned and fall short of the glory of God..." Quite a different assessment of the human race from that which we as human beings often have of ourselves, is this not? But why would God have such an assessment of the whole human race? For the answer to that question, we need to be aware that God is Creator of all that exists, so that when God created the first man, Adam, at the beginning of time, God created him in innocence, meaning that Adam as first created by God neither knew good nor evil, nor was there any sin anywhere in God's original sinless creation.

However, the day came when God tested Adam with a command, saying to him in the garden of Eden here on earth, which was the perfect environment which God had for him, what we now read at Genesis 2:16,17, "[16] The Lord God commanded the man, saying, "From any tree of the garden you may eat freely; [17] but from the tree of the knowledge of good and evil you shall not eat, for in the day that you eat from it you will surely die." How important to see here that God gave Adam, who although a real person was also representative of the whole human race, the warning of the penalty of death for disobedience to His command.

Unfortunately, the day did come when Adam did partake of the forbidden tree and thereby did sin against God. The moment that happened, Adam not only became a sinner by practice, but also a sinner by nature. One thing my parents had to continually do while under their care was to restrain me from continually going the wrong way, for it seemed that of myself I could not do good, but kept going into sin. The reason this was happening is that from the age of accountability onwards, I had not only become a sinner by practice, but also a sinner by nature.

And here the age of accountability needs to be seen as being when as a young child in innocence – which moment is known only by God – one comes to learn the right from the wrong and chooses the wrong, thereby becoming personally accountable to God for one's own sin against Him, since all sin is first of all against Him. And that is why God can say at Romans 3:23 above that "all have sinned and fall short of the glory of God," because God knows that all human beings will go the way of Adam, our representative man, which is also why God can say what He does in regards to the whole of the human race at Romans 5:12, where we read, "Therefore, just as through one man (Adam) sin entered into the world, and death through sin, and so death spread to all men, because all sinned" (from the age of accountability onward). And so, we see that the whole human race is declared by God to not only be sinners by practice and by nature from the age of accountability onwards, but the whole of the human race is now subject to death! In other words, in God's sight the whole of the human race is under the judgment of the penalty of death, due to all being sinners by practice and by nature.

You will recall above, in the first verse we quoted from Romans 6:23, God did say there that "the wages of sin is death." And what God means by "death" here is not just loss of physical life, as when the physical body we have dies; but also has spiritual death in mind, which is far worse! Spiritual death has its beginning when a separation takes place between a person and God at the moment one becomes a sinner at the age of accountability and ends after the final judgment of time, when God forever casts away from His Presence those who before physical death refused to believe in His Son, The Lord Jesus Christ, thereby personally forfeiting the forgiveness of their sins and eternal life with God. And now all such will pay the penalty for their own sins in hell, away from the Presence of God forever.

It is in the midst of such a hopeless situation in which the whole of the human race found itself in that God TOOK THE INITIATIVE and sent His own eternally existing Son into the world, as born of a virgin in the innocence of Adam – so as not to inherit the sinful nature passed on from generation after generation from Adam onwards through the conception of the female – so that He might be the acceptable sacrifice offered to God His Father at the cross, there bearing our sins in His body, and there dying the death due our sins! God's Son, Jesus Christ, was then buried and raised from the dead the third day, to ever be alive, for it is through Him, on the basis of what God has done for us through His Son, that God The Father forgives our sins and imparts us eternal life.

Now, by God's grace and His enablement, may you see your need of God's Son to be Your Savior from the penalty due sin, which is death, not only physical, but also spiritual. And by God's grace, may He lead you to believe in His Son, Jesus Christ, and in believing, to receive the forgiveness of your sins and eternal life with God forever! And based on the truth just shared, the author would now like to ask you a few questions, with the answer being just between yourself and God:

When God says at Romans 3:23, "for all have sinned and fall short of the glory of God," does that include you?

When God says at Romans 5:8, "But God demonstrates His own love toward us, in that while we were yet sinners, Christ died for us," were you included in Christ's death on behalf of sinners?

And when God further says at 1 Peter 3:18 in part, "For Christ also died for sins once for all, the just for the unjust, so that He might bring us to God, having been put to death in the flesh, but made alive in the spirit," were you part of the unjust for whom Christ died?

When God says at Romans 6:23, "For the wages of sin is death, but the free gift of God is eternal life in Christ Jesus our Lord," do you want that eternal life as a free gift from God?

When God says at John 3:16, "For God so loved the world, that He gave His only begotten Son, that whoever believes in Him shall not perish, but have eternal life," do you now believe that Jesus Christ is indeed God's Son in human flesh, Who came from Heaven to this earth to die in your place, so as to save you from ever experiencing the judgment of God leading to an eternal separation from God in hell?

And when God then further says to you at Isaiah 55:6, "Seek the Lord while He may be found; call upon Him while He is near," for His further promise to you here is as we read at Romans 10:9-11,13, "[9] that if you confess with your mouth Jesus as Lord, and believe in your heart that God raised Him from the dead, you will be saved (that is, you will now enter into a personal relationship with God by faith); [10] for with the heart a person believes, resulting in righteousness (that is, in now receiving God's own righteous and eternal life to live by), and with the mouth he confesses, resulting in salvation (that is, in now receiving as a free gift the forgiveness of sins and eternal life with God). [11] For the Scripture says, “Whoever believes in Him will not be disappointed…” [13] for “Whoever will call on the name of the Lord will be saved.” Will you now call upon God from your heart to save you?

The author’s prayer for you at this point, as you now call upon God by His grace, is what we read at Romans 15:13, “Now may the God of hope fill you with all joy and peace in believing, so that you will abound in hope by the power of the Holy Spirit.”

The next book

As this book is being published, God has given His servant the go-ahead to write another book, titled "God's Prophetic Word Through Joel, Zephaniah, and Habakkuk."

Since the author's two websites are no longer active, one may access the books, and places to purchase, by typing "Roger Henri Trepanier, books" in any search engine.

If you have found this book profitable, or any other of the author's books, please feel free to let family, friends, and co-workers know about this book and the other books. The author is not on any social media sites, so he relies on God and readers to spread the word. May God bless you for doing so!

Made in the USA
Middletown, DE
05 December 2024